The
PASTA-LOVER'S DIET BOOK

by June Roth, M.S.

he Bobbs-Merrill Company, Inc.   Indianapolis / New York

To Mother and Dad
with deepest love and appreciation
for your warm and constant devotion

Copyright © 1984 by June Roth

Published by The Bobbs-Merrill Company, Inc.
Indianapolis/New York

Manufactured in the United States of America

Second Printing

Designed by Sheila Lynch
Drawings Courtesy of the National Pasta Association

Library of Congress Cataloging in Publication Data

Roth, June Spiewak.
The pasta lover's diet book.

Includes indexes.
1. Low-calorie diet—Recipes. 2. Salt-free diet—Recipes.
3. Cookery (Macaroni)
I. Title.
RM 222.2.R678   1984   641.5′635   83-15571

Contents

Dear Reader:

The only time when being a loser means you are actually a winner is when you are playing the diet game. The more unwanted fat you lose, the more you win in good looks and good health.

Despite your desire to lose accumulated pounds with some miraculous plan, it makes no sense to gamble with your body chemistry by embarking on a fad diet. You can really do more damage than good if your daily intake isn't well balanced and rich in the nutrients you need to function well.

But there is a way to lose weight that fills your own body image desires and yet accomplishes meeting your biochemical needs. Strange as it seems, it makes use of pasta, a food that you may have avoided because you thought it was a no-no for a weight-loss diet. Actually, when eaten in moderate portions with low-calorie sauces, it can be a way to make you a lucky loser.

Just as you ate the weight on, you are going to have to eat it off. My aim with this book is to show you a way to eat it off without starving and with some measure of gustatorial pleasure. The word is out that pasta is in for those who want to be thin!

Warmly,
JUNE ROTH

One

Dieting Can Be a Pleasure

The trouble with most diets is that they seem to punish you with a pattern of foods that you don't really want to eat. Let's face it, people who have to diet are generally people who enjoy the pleasure of eating. They need a feeling of satiation. Hunger pangs destroy their happy vibes. In order to lose weight, there is need for a diet that is interesting, filling, fun, delicious, and nutritious. That's what the Pasta-Lover's Diet is all about!

Far from being fattening, pasta scores a mere 210 calories per 5-ounce cooked serving (made from 2 ounces of uncooked pasta) without sauce. The trick is to keep the sauces low caloried as well, to be able to eat enough to be comfortable while losing weight. The recipes in this book have been devised to let you enjoy mealtimes with a variety of pasta dishes and skinnied down sauces while dieting your way to a slimmer YOU.

You'll find a two-week diet menu that spells out each meal's ingredients, to help you to have a good balance of nutrition each day. Substitution lists will help you when you are dining in restaurants, so you won't be tempted to go off the diet. But if you do, don't despair. Just get back on it the very next meal and don't worry about it. Your excess weight didn't go on in a day or a week and it won't

1

come off and stay off on a starvation regime. The Pasta-Lover's Diet is designed to please your palate while skillfully removing calories that you don't need to eat. The variety of pasta dishes should keep you well fed and amused enough to anticipate each meal with pleasure, while you slowly and safely drop those pounds of stored fat.

While the menus are designed for a two-week diet, you can safely stay with this eating regimen for as long as you wish. Each meal and each day have been carefully evaluated to give you a totally nutritious combination of ingredients that will keep you in optimum health.

You will find a chapter of breakfast combinations that will give you a good start to your day. Skipping breakfast is a foolhardy dieter's habit: Cars don't run without gas and people don't function well without necessary fuel. At any rate, those who try to fool Mother Nature by skipping meals only succeed in eating more at the next meal. The starve-and-gorge yo-yo syndrome is what gets people into bad eating habits that lead to overweight. Better to eat three evenly paced calorie meals to help you to maintain a regular pattern of energy and vitality.

Lunches will have vegetable sauces, low-calorie cheese sauces, and pseudo-cream sauces. Each recipe will have suggested vegetable accompaniments so your meal will always be in excellent nutritious balance.

Dinners will feature pasta dishes that have fish, chicken, and meat in the sauce or filling. Again, vegetable accompaniments will be suggested to round out your vitamin and mineral intake. Salads will be featured with tasty low-calorie dressings that are easy to make and store in the refrigerator. These are not the tasteless gluey kind that are made commercially, but rather a combination of juices, vinegars, seasonings, and herbs that give a zestful lift to raw vegetable combinations without drowning them in goop.

And finally, although you will be eating a mere 1000 calories each day to help you to lose up to two or three pounds a week, you will be able to enjoy one pleasant dessert at dinnertime that will take the punishment out of dieting. A chapter of such easy and delicious desserts that are low in calories is provided for your indulgence.

Each pound of stored fat on your body represents 3,500 calories that you did not burn up. It can sneak on easily via 500 extra calories a day that add up to a pound of excess intake each week. Simple mathematics reveals that if you keep up that kind of excess intake for a year, you will have added fifty pounds unintentionally. Fortunately, most people have weeks of lethargy and overeating and then other weeks of activity and burning up their intake. So the stored fat may only total fifteen or twenty-five pounds that you don't want or need.

The basis for losing weight is to eat 500 calories less each day to lose a pound a week, or 1,000 calories less each day if you want to lose a desirable two pounds a week. Naturally, there is a point at which your body must have essential nutrients to give energy, and to repair the bone structure and collagen connective tissues that are in a constant state of regrowth. The trick, therefore, is to feed your body well with high-density nutrients, making every mouthful count for excellence in vitamin and mineral content, while satisfying your appetite at the same time. This can be done at the 1,000-calorie-per-day level, if the menus are structured skillfully. When you go below that point, you are literally taking your life and health in your hands!

Do discuss this diet with your medical doctor and have a checkup before you start. It is wise to be under the care of your doctor throughout the weight-loss period to be sure that you are not losing weight too rapidly. Be sure to get blood cholesterol and triglyceride testing before and after the diet. Eating the moderate-protein, low-fat, high-complex-carbohydrate way should bring both factors into normal ranges if your first test reveals high levels of one or both.

You are about to embark on an adventure of dieting and eating wonderful-tasting food. It is not a fad diet, but rather one that is based on the biochemical needs of the human body. The object is to help you to slim down with satiety and sense.

Now if you have no real knowledge of the basic facts of nutrition and why pasta is good for you, please read the following chapter slowly and carefully so you can understand what makes this diet both fun and sensible at the same time.

Two

Facts of
Sensible Diet Nutrition

What the world needs now is hardly another diet book to tell you how to lose weight steadily and comfortably. And yet, some people need a plan that is based on good nutrition and that can be relied upon to deliver a loss of weight without ruining the body's delicate balancing system. What good is a slim figure if the price you pay for it is a lifetime of poor health?

Fortunately, most dieters usually cannot adhere to the diets prescribed by many so-called experts who recommend bizarre food combinations and promise hefty body weight reductions, without an educated knowledge of how the intricate absorption and metabolic pathways function. The reason the usual weight-loss diet that is started on Monday morning fails by Tuesday afternoon is that it is too depriving, too rigid, and too boring. It doesn't have to be that way. If you learn how to streamline the fat and sugar out of food to reduce your intake to a mere 1,000 calories a day, that food can be of high-density nutrition, have great variety, and still tickle your taste buds. This book is going to show you how to lose weight the healthful and pleasurable way!

The first step is to forget that pasta has heretofore been a forbidden food on weight-loss diets. This was due to the mistaken notion that carbohydrates and "starchy foods" were the enemy of dieting efforts. They were called "fattening" although they did not have fat (the real culprit!) in them except for the butter, cream, bacon, etc., that was added to the carbohydrate food.

Therefore, dieters who were afraid to eat carbohydrates thought it safe to load up on high-protein foods which can cause stress to the kidneys when taken in excess. Protein can also provide more calories than needed because of the interweaving of fat throughout most high-protein foods. The next time you see a piece of raw beef, examine the fat graining throughout the meat and the wedges of pure fat that surround each cut. Take a look at the fat lurking under poultry skin. Taste the difference between high-fat content cheese and low-fat content cheese. Notice the contrast between a glass of skim milk and a glass of whole milk. The hidden fat content may surprise you!

All food, as you probably know, provides three major nutrients: protein, fats, and carbohydrates. Whatever you eat has to be one or more of these categories. In addition, whatever you eat has vitamin and mineral values that must be considered. A simple way to know that you are getting a variety of such vitamins and minerals is to eat colorful food—reds, yellows, orange, light green, dark green, purple, brown, and white—on every possible plate. The more variety of different foods you eat, the more variety of vitamins and minerals you will be ingesting. That is why the recipes and menus in this book have an unusual amount of variation and color. Certainly, it will be visually attractive to you, but also it will be the kind of healthful combination of food that your body requires in order to thrive.

Of the three categories of food, protein contains 4.0 calories per gram of food intake. Rich sources of protein are meat, fish, poultry, dairy products, nuts, and legumes when combined with a grain (such as beans and rice combinations). Unfortunately, a good part of the protein that we eat is interwoven with animal fat. Fat contains double the calories of protein, or 9 calories per gram of food ingested. Fat stays in your stomach longer, is digested slower, and is absorbed leisurely through the small intestine. That's why fat gives you a feeling of well-being and satiety when eaten. You do need some fat in your daily intake, but it can be limited if you avoid butter, margarine, high-fat content cheese, mayonnaise-type dressings and add just a teaspoon of vegetable oil to your salad each day. All fat contains about 100 calories per tablespoon. Animal fats are called "saturated fat," while vegetable-based fats are "unsaturated" or "low-cholesterol" fats.

It is possible to lower the amount of fat that is connected to the protein you eat, if you carefully select lean meats, such as veal, lean cuts of beef, poultry without the skin, increased amounts of fish, and skim milk dairy products. You can assume that you will take in enough saturated fats despite your precautions, and that all other fats should be eaten in the form of unsaturated fats.

If you eat 12 percent of your daily intake in protein, as is recommended by sensible medical practitioners, nutritionists, and the United States revised Dietary Goals, you are left with 88 percent of the menu to fill with fats and carbohydrates. While most Americans have increased their fat intake to 45 percent and over, it is highly recommended that this be reduced to between 20 and 30 percent at most.

Let's go back to simple mathematics. If you eat 12 percent protein each day and 20 to 30 percent fat each day, this leaves you between 58 and 68 percent for carbohydrates. And that is exactly what the knowledgeable health experts are recommending that you revise your diet to include. Carbohydrates have the same 4.0 calories per gram as does protein, and, thus, both have half as many calories as fat.

The problem with eating a high-carbohydrate diet is that most people don't understand that there are different classifications of carbohydrates. They lump them all as sweets and starches, and we have all been taught that these are bad. Not so! Sugars, syrups, and honey are simple carbohydrates. They are absorbed quickly into the system and tend to push the blood sugar levels up too fast. You feel great when the sugar level goes up; then you go on a roller coaster of feelings when the sugar level goes down just as swiftly. You may have a headache, you may feel depressed, or you may just feel that you're dragging. You seem to need another sugar "fix" at that time to get you through the next few hours. This explains the effect of the coffee break that often consists of a sweetened beverage and a sweet doughnut or piece of Danish pastry—just enough sugar to send your blood sugar level soaring again. It's better to stay on an even keel with a slower source of energy keeping you at a steady mood and work level. You don't need the simple sugars. They are contained in large quantities with fats in cakes, cookies, pies, ice cream, and other desserts and snack foods.

Sugar and fat together in these products give you nothing but empty calories that are stored as triglycerides in warehouses on your hips. These triglycerides are the body's backup system for energy. They can be backpedaled into the glucose metabolism pathways if needed. The problem is that people who have built up huge storage areas of triglycerides just keep adding to the storage depots and never get to use up the surplus. In other words, they get fatter and fatter because any excess caloric intake is not burned off each day.

On the other hand, whole grains, vegetables, and fruits are complex carbohydrates that give you steady sources of energy throughout the day for comparatively low calories. They also are a source of high fiber in the diet when they are not refined, overcooked, and puréed. If you can get the knack of taking in just as many complex carbohydrates as you will burn off through the day, you will not store any excess. If you increase your exercise program, you can take in more carbohydrates. If you run in marathons, you'll even learn how to "load" carbohydrates for storage in your muscle tissue before the event, to be able to convert it to instant energy as needed. The recipes in this book are geared to those people who do not exercise regularly and, thus, must be on a limited intake to contribute to the energy pool as it is needed, but not to create an ocean of energy potential that will never be used.

It is very important to be aware of this exercise information when you are dieting to lose weight. Calculate that you will burn off 100 calories for every mile of walking, bicycling, or swimming that you do—roughly, half an hour of activity. Two miles will mean you have used up 200 calories. If you are eating to maintain your weight, that entitles you to eat an extra 200 calories per day. If you are eating to maintain your health and lose weight, don't eat any more, and let the exercise speed you on your way to further weight loss. This simple explanation may make you think that if you ate only 800 calories a day and didn't exercise, you would be in the same place—but you'd be wrong! Indeed, you would be at the 800-calorie level of intake, but you would have taken in 200 calories less of nutrients which you cannot afford to do if you are interested in good health. Fuel the body properly and you will be practicing preventive medicine. The 1,000 calories of high-density nutrients must be eaten, digested, and offered to the metabolic systems of the body in order to maintain the system that is so intricately dependent on a wide variety of food intake.

For a quick grasp of the vitamin content of complex carbohydrates (refined simple sugar carbohydrates have lost these values) learn them by color:

Vitamin A is found in the yellow, orange, red, and dark green fruits and vegetables.

Vitamin C is found in the light green vegetables, citrus fruits, and bright red fruits and vegetables (strawberries, tomatoes, red peppers) and in white potatoes.

Vitamin B's are found in red meat, organ meats, yeast, green leafy vegetables, whole grain cereals, breads, and pasta.

Vitamin D is found in fish liver oils, fortified milk, and in the rays of the sun.

Vitamin E is found in plant tissues, such as in wheat germ oil, vegetable oils, nuts, and legumes.

Vitamin K is found in green leaves of spinach, cabbage, cauliflower, and in liver.

Here is a summary of the recommended patterning for your best nutritional intake:

CURRENT AMERICAN DIET	RECOMMENDED DIET
12 percent protein	12 percent protein
42 percent fat	20 to 30 percent fat
46 percent carbohydrates	58 to 68 percent carbohydrates
(22 percent complex carbohydrates and 24 percent simple carbohydrates)	(53 to 63 percent complex carbohydrates and 5 to 10 percent simple carbohydrates)

Increased complex carbohydrates in the form of whole grains, vegetables, and fruits will give you the variety you require. You can ruin the good effects of these complex carbohydrates by saucing them with butter or cream, or sugaring the fruits that don't need it. In general, our taste buds have become so used to these excessive slatherings that add nothing but empty calories to the diet that we have lost our sensitivity to enjoy simple, well prepared food.

Pasta is a good carbohydrate food. It is also low in sodium, often providing only 1 milligram of sodium per cooked cup of pasta. Since overweight people often suffer from fluid retention, and reduced sodium intake can be helpful in overcoming this problem, low-sodium foods are important when dieting and maintaining good health. The body requires about 2,500 mg. of sodium to keep in balance. Interestingly, that is just about the amount of natural sodium that is contained in the meats, fish, poultry, vegetables, fruits, and grains we eat—without adding a grain of salt from the shaker. In this book, you will find a minimum of sodium used to season foods. Instead, there will be a wide array of herbs and spices to give superb taste sensations without adding any calories.

Now that you have learned the sensible biochemical and nutritional premise of this book, you are ready to learn more about how pasta can play a major role in helping you to lose weight and to keep it off. Yes, you can eat smart to stay healthy and yet lose excess weight!

Three

The Varieties of Pasta

Most people think of spaghetti or macaroni when the word "pasta" is mentioned. Indeed, these are among the favorite varieties of pasta that exist. But to limit yourself to these is to miss half the fun of exploring the many shapes and textures available as commercially made pasta.

The best way to discover the kinds of pasta that are ready to cook is to walk down the aisle of your supermarket and explore the possibilities. You will find flat linguini, wide lasagne noodles, bows, spirals, and tubes of every size and length. Spaghetti will be there in regular and thin forms, and macaroni will prevail in short straight form or elbows of every size.

The official estimate of the National Pasta Association is that 150 different shapes prevail, but a manufacturer of metal dies used to produce macaroni shapes claims that a total of 325 shapes could be made in this country. You may not be able to find all of them, but they do fall into general categories that you might find fun to try.

Spaghetti, for instance, is a general term used for the solid, rod form of macaroni. Round rods may be made in any of 16 different diameters, ranging from *fedelini* (the smallest) up through *capellini, vermicelli, spaghettini, spaghetti,* and finally to *spaghettoni,* which is the largest size. Some solid rods are made in an oval shape, with *bavettine* being the smallest, followed by *bavette*, then *linguini*, and finally *linguini di passeri*. The flat forms of pasta are known as noodles. Among these in the long form are the very narrow *trenettine, trenette, fettuccelle, fettuccine, fettucce, lasagnette,* and the wide *lasagne*. Altogether, there are about 14 different sizes in this group. Some of these may be called egg noodles, and may be designated as narrow or fine, medium, wide, or broad. Some may be extra long and called "folded." *Fettuccine* means "ribbons" in Italian, aptly describing many of these flat shapes.

Many times the flat shapes have variations. They may be curly on one side, known as *fettuccelle riccie un lato*. Altogether there could be as many as 11 such flat shapes that are curly on one side, with names that echo the other flat noodles. More shapes can be added to the list with those flat shapes that are made curly on both sides. In this group, from small to large, are *mafaldine, mafalda, lasagnette riccie, lasagne riccie,* and *lasagne large riccie,* with the larger ones known simply as *lasagne*.

A third group of macaroni products contains round products with holes in the middle. This variety is almost uncountable. The smooth ones alone have about 20 possible sizes, including tiny *spaghetti bucati,* followed by *bucatini, perciatelli, macheroncelli, mezzanelli, mezzani, ziti, zitoni, occhio di lupo, canelle,* and the very large *tufoli*. To complicate matters when trying to identify the pasta with accuracy, many round products with holes are also made with ridges, starting from the small *perciatelli,* to the larger *cannelle,* then the *rigati,* and finally the *rigatoni*. In this group there is a possibility of 41 macaroni products that can be made in a long form.

When these hollow tubular forms are cut into short lengths, and the lengths are varied, another number of pasta possibilities arise. About 14 kinds of smooth tubes are made longer than the familiar elbow macaroni. These generally have the term *magliette* coming before names already given to the hollow shapes. The tubes with ridges that are cut into shorter lengths appear in 28 more shapes, with the term *rigati* tacked on at the end.

Elbow macaroni products come in 11 sizes, depending on the diameter, and 8 of these may be made with ridges. If the macaroni is made without the "elbow" curve, it can be cut in shorter lengths, providing 9 more sizes. For example, *bucatini* cut in very short lengths become *tubettini;* macaroni similarly cut is called *ditalini* (salad macaroni).

Other well known and popular forms of pasta are smooth and ridged shells, ranging from very small to very large in size—in all about 13 possible sizes. There are also alphabets made in two sizes, and about 84 special fancy products such as *anelli rigati* (ridged rings), *stellini* (small star), crowns, hearts, clubs, spades, diamonds, melon seeds, and very tiny *pastina.*

Finally there are about 27 other pasta shapes, including round and square wheels, *cavatelli, creste de galli* (cockscombs) triangles, fish, *fusilli* (twisted *spaghetti bucatini*), *yolanda* and *margherita* (two more twisted types), and *riccini* (curls).

These pasta products seem to fall into two categories: Those you boil and sauce, and those you bake in sauce. Many of the baked varieties are first parboiled and stuffed before being sauced and baked in the oven. However you choose to prepare pasta, it is always easy and quick to cook and a popular item to serve. Here's a quick guide to the best ways to use the main types of macaroni, spaghetti, and egg noodles:

Elbow macaroni, shells, corkscrew macaroni, bows, and other shapes of about the same size:
Use in casseroles, salads, soups, and stews.

Spaghetti of various sizes, fusilli (twisted spaghetti), linguine (flat spaghetti):
Use with meat, poultry, vegetable, fish, or cheese sauces.

Egg noodles (fine, medium, or wide):
   Use with sauces or in casseroles, soups, or desserts.

Pastina and other very small shapes:
   Use in soups and for children's meals.

If you are an accomplished cook and love to putter in the kitchen, you should consider making your own pasta. You can use an electric pasta-maker that whirls the dough together and then presses it through disks and forms it into the shapes you select. Or you can make your own dough by hand or in a food processor and feed it through a hand-operated pasta machine to produce lovely linguini, spaghetti, or lasagne.

While most commercial pasta is made without eggs, except for egg noodles, homemade pasta is best when it includes an egg. Be sure to allow the dough to rest for 10 to 20 minutes before rolling it through a pasta machine or even by hand with a rolling pin. Here's a recipe that works well for homemade pasta:

   2 cups unbleached all-purpose flour
   2 eggs
   ¼ teaspoon salt
   up to 1 tablespoon cold water

If mixing the dough by hand, put the flour on a board and make a well in the center. Break the eggs into the well and beat them lightly with a fork. Gradually work the eggs into the flour from the sides of the well until all is combined. Add salt as you are working it all together into a smooth dough. If the dough is too stiff, add up to 1 tablespoon cold water and knead well. Then let the dough rest before rolling and cutting it.

To make the dough in a food processor, merely place all the ingredients into the container and turn on the processor. The dough should form a smooth lump and clear the sides of the container. If not, a bit more water may be needed.

To make spinach dough, chop enough fresh spinach to make ½ cup, or thaw frozen chopped spinach, drain it well, and add ½ cup to the dough.

The mistake that most people make when cooking pasta is not to use a large enough pot and enough water to let the pasta separate naturally during the boiling. Follow the directions on the package for commercially purchased pasta, using 6 quarts of water for each pound of pasta to be cooked. If you intend to add a bit of salt, do so just before adding the pasta. It is not necessary to add oil to the cooking water if you use the 6 quarts of water that are recommended. When cooking homemade pasta, test strands constantly: the cooking time is much shorter for this than for commercially made pasta.

Bring the water to a rapid boil before adding the pasta. As you add the pasta, be sure that the water continues to boil. The rapid and continuous boiling helps to keep the pasta moving about so it will cook quickly and evenly. Cook it uncovered, stirring occasionally and gently, until the pasta is tender. Stirring helps to keep the pasta evenly distributed and moving in the boiling water so that all of it will be cooked at the same time.

Test for doneness by tasting a piece of the pasta. Many people prefer pasta tender, yet firm—a condition the Italians call "*al dente.*" Cooking time will vary with the size and thickness of the pasta product you are using. Very small pasta products may cook in 2 minutes, while some large shapes may require 15 minutes. Cook the pasta a little shorter time if it is going to be used in a casserole and receive further cooking.

Those who insist upon eating spaghetti *al dente* should realize that it adds about 40 calories to each cupful. The more tender the spaghetti, the lower the calorie count, as some of the calories tend to escape into the cooking water. When the pasta is done, drain at once and toss it with some sauce to keep the strands from sticking together. If you get into the habit of having your sauce ready before you begin to cook the pasta, you'll have no trouble with the timing or keeping the strands separated. Baked pasta may be kept warming for a while, but don't do that to boiled pasta, which should be served immediately. Never rinse pasta unless you are planning to use it for a cold salad—otherwise use sauce to keep the strands from sticking together.

If you have leftover cooked pasta, it may be refrigerated for several days until ready to use it. Add it during the last 5 minutes of cooking soup, or use it in a salad, or add it to eggs when scrambling them for an omelet (use about ½ cup for each egg used). Leftover pasta can also be reheated by dropping it into boiling water for a few minutes until the pasta is heated through.

To measure uncooked pasta quickly, it helps to know that 4 ounces of uncooked spaghetti held in a bundle will fill a circle the size of a quarter, and 4 ounces of uncooked macaroni will fill a cup. To be more accurate, use a kitchen scale until you get the knack of measuring by eye.

There's a wonderful world of pasta choices waiting for you. Here are some drawings which will help you to recognize the great variety of available pasta:

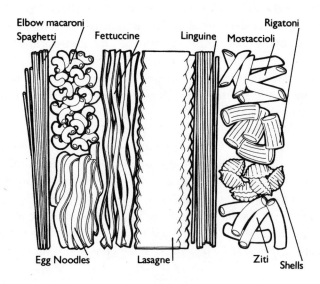

Four

Basics of the Pasta-Lover's Diet

There are several reasons why you would want to lose weight with a diet that permitted delicious portions of pasta at two meals a day. One is that it sounds downright "naughty" to someone who has considered pasta to be forbidden on any weight-loss diet. Another is that it might be a fun way to lose weight. Actually, it's a sensible and filling way to approach the task of dropping some excess stored fat, and will give you the opportunity to enjoy the experience. While the menu plan outlines a two-week regimen of about 1,000 calories a day, this way of eating can be continued for as long as you wish. Do check with your doctor before embarking on this or any low-calorie diet to be sure that it is suitable for you.

The premise of the *Pasta-Lover's Diet Book* is to eat a well-balanced and filling low-calorie diet. The daily combinations have been designed for the person who likes to cook and wants to make something special for each meal. If you eat in restaurants some or all of the time, or you are not inclined to cook all your meals, you may want to make some substitutions in the menus. Here's how to follow the diet and yet make whatever changes you desire.

BREAKFASTS: Always have ½ cup of juice or berries or melon to start. Always have either 1 egg prepared without fat (boiled, poached, or scrambled in a nonstick frying pan), or a sugar-free cereal with skim milk. For a hot beverage, you may choose regular or decaffeinated coffee or tea, using only skim milk with it. Do not add sugar to your beverage. Consult the calorie counter in the back of the book and write down everything you do eat when you vary the prescribed menu. The calories should add up to about 1,000 a day.

LUNCHES: Always try to have 2 ounces of dried pasta cooked (cooked it becomes 5 ounces or about 1 cup) with a vegetable sauce. This may be half a cup of a commercially prepared tomato sauce, marinara sauce, or meatless spaghetti sauce, if desired. Avoid any sauce that has been prepared with fat or oil because you will be defeating the purpose of this diet, which is to cut down on your fat intake. Do not add salt to your food as sodium retains fluid and makes it more difficult to lose weight. You may sprinkle 1 table-spoon of grated Parmesan cheese over the cooked pasta. Always have either a mixed green salad or a low-calorie cooked vegetable. At home, use one of the suggested recipes for low-calorie dressings or a commercially bottled low-calorie dressing on your salad. Use 1 tablespoon of dressing per serving and toss well to coat. Otherwise use a flavored vinegar, such as tarragon vinegar, or lemon juice.

DINNERS: Notice that all of the pasta recipes with meat, poultry, or fish sauces use a minimum amount—just enough to give you the protein you require. When you're in a hurry at home, you can make the Mini-Meat Sauce or brown 3 ounces of lean ground beef or veal and add to a commercial tomato sauce. Each pasta dish should be accompanied by low-calorie cooked vegetables or a mixed salad with a low-calorie dressing. When dining in a restaurant, if the portion of pasta is too large, push the excess aside. One cup of cooked pasta is the rule to follow, along with a 3-ounce portion of meat, poultry, or fish in the sauce or alongside the pasta. Choose melon, berries, half a grapefruit, or a fresh fruit salad for dessert.

OTHER TIPS: Choose whole grain breads when indicated for breakfast. Add a tablespoon of wheat germ to cereal or sprinkle it on one of your salads for 28 calories of B-complex vitamins. When friends are drinking cocktails, have a slice of lime in a glass of sparkling water. If hunger pangs attack before bedtime, you can have a whole orange, but peel it very, very slowly. Have celery sticks cleaned and chilling in the refrigerator for moments when munching is a must. (Theoretically, you use up 2 calories more by chewing than you actually eat of the celery.) If you need to binge, choose unbuttered, unsalted popcorn at 23 calories per cupful.

RESTAURANT SUBSTITUTIONS: It's rare for a restaurant not to be able to accommodate your request for a simple pasta dish. That's the beauty of a food beloved by all. However, if it happens at lunchtime, you may choose a tuna salad sandwich on one slice of whole wheat bread or in a pita pocket. Have a portion of coleslaw with it. Skip the pickle; it's loaded with salt! For dinner, choose a small piece of broiled fish (no butter), two cooked low-calorie vegetables (green beans, asparagus, broccoli, spinach, zucchini, etc.), or one vegetable and a mixed green salad with lemon or vinegar for dressing. Choose tomato juice or bouillon for starters, and have melon or berries for dessert.

EXERCISE: You must get moving! (With your doctor's approval, of course.) Build up to walking a mile briskly. Every mile you walk will burn up 100 calories. A good goal is to walk two miles every day of your life. Other exercises that work well are jogging, swimming, biking, aerobic dancing, and jumping rope. Choose one form of exercise that fits your life-style and make it part of your day's activities. Skip the elevators and climb the stairs. Skip the coffee breaks and take a walk, even if it's in a long hallway. Change your body's sluggish sedentary habits and wake up every muscle by stretching, bending, and moving as much as possible.

Notice that the 14 days of menus offer a wide variety of foods, textures, flavors, and colors. You will have a feeling of comfortable satiety from the amount of complex carbohydrates you will be eating. Now, at last, here's a diet that will show you how to take it off the smart nutritious way!

1,000 CALORIE BASIC MENU PLAN

BREAKFAST: Choice of unsweetened fruit juice, half a grapefruit, half a sliced orange, melon wedge, or fresh berries in season.

Choice of poached, boiled, or scrambled egg without use of fat in cooking, with 1 slice toasted whole grain bread; or choice of a hot or cold unsweetened cereal with skim milk and ½ sliced banana, if desired; or ½ cup low-fat cottage cheese with 1 slice toasted whole grain bread.

LUNCH: 5 ounces cooked pasta (no oil in the boiling water, no butter after draining) with plain tomato sauce or other low-calorie vegetable sauce.

Choice of two low-calorie vegetables or one vegetable and a mixed green salad with a low-calorie dressing.

DINNER: 3 ounces of meat, poultry, or fish in a low-calorie pasta sauce on 5 ounces cooked pasta (no oil in the boiling water, no butter after draining).

Choice of a low-calorie cooked vegetable or a mixed green salad with a low-calorie dressing.

Choice of an apple or pear (raw, poached, or baked with no sugar added), or ½ cup any water-packed fruit, melon wedge, or ½ cup fresh berries in season. On occasion, ¼ cup frozen yogurt or iced milk may be served on a water-packed pear or peach half.

BEVERAGES: Choice of coffee, decaffeinated coffee, or tea with skim milk, no sugar (artificial sweetener if desired).

SNACKS: Celery or carrot sticks, unbuttered, unsalted popcorn (1 cup), lime wedge in sparkling water, 1 small orange (limited to 1 a day).

SEASONINGS: Unlimited use of herbs and spices. Oil is limited to 1 teaspoon daily on a salad. No added salt, and no pickles or packaged food products. No added sugar, and no butter or cream. (Use only skim milk products.)

FOURTEEN-DAY MENU PLAN

In this section all recipes marked with asterisks can be found in this book. Check the index for the page numbers.

DAY 1

BREAKFAST: ½ grapefruit
French Toast*
Coffee, decaffeinated coffee, or tea

LUNCH: Spaghetti with Fresh Tomato–Cucumber Sauce*
½ cup cooked spinach
Coffee, decaffeinated coffee, or tea

DINNER: Beef–Noodle Ragout*
Green salad with sliced radishes and low-calorie
dressing
½ cup unsweetened applesauce

DAY 2

BREAKFAST: ½ cup orange juice
               ½ cup raisin bran cereal
               ½ banana, sliced
               ½ cup skim milk
               Coffee, Decaffeinated coffee, or tea

LUNCH: Fettucini Almost–Alfredo*
               ½ cup cooked chopped broccoli
               ½ cup cooked sliced carrots
               Coffee, decaffeinated coffee, or tea

DINNER: Chicken Cacciatore on Linguini*
               Mixed green salad with low-calorie dressing
               ½ cup unsweetened sliced pears
               Coffee, decaffeinated coffee, or tea

DAY 3

BREAKFAST: ½ cup unsweetened pineapple juice
               Cheese Danish*
               Coffee, decaffeinated coffee, or tea

LUNCH: Spaghetti and Mushrooms Marinara*
               Mixed green salad with sliced cucumbers and
                   low-calorie dressing
               Coffee, decaffeinated coffee, or tea

DINNER: ½ cup tomato juice with a lemon wedge
               Shish Kebab and Linguini Pesto*
               ½ cup cooked zucchini
               Frozen Fresh Fruit Purée*
               Coffee, decaffeinated coffee, or tea

DAY 4

BREAKFAST: ½ cup orange juice
                    Baked Egg in English Muffin*
                    Coffee, decaffeinated coffee, or tea

LUNCH: Pasta Twists with Broccoli Sauce*
                    Mixed green salad with grated carrot and low-calorie dressing
                    Coffee, decaffeinated coffee, or tea

DINNER: 1 cup clear bouillon
                    Spaghetti with One Meatball*
                    ½ cup cooked spinach
                    Crisp green salad with low-calorie dressing
                    Melon wedge
                    Coffee, decaffeinated coffee, or tea

DAY 5

BREAKFAST: ½ sliced orange
                    Grits with Almonds*
                    Coffee, decaffeinated coffee, or tea

LUNCH: Spaghetti and Mushrooms Marinara*
                    Crisp green salad with sliced cucumbers and low-calorie dressing
                    Coffee, decaffeinated coffee, or tea

DINNER: Poached Fish Rolls on Noodles*
                    ½ cup cooked zucchini
                    ½ cup Crisp Cabbage Salad*
                    ½ cup strawberries
                    Coffee, decaffeinated coffee, or tea

DAY 6

BREAKFAST: ½ grapefruit
Jelly Roll Omelet*
Coffee, decaffeinated coffee, or tea

LUNCH: Ziti with Mushroom–Pepper Sauce*
Mixed raw vegetable salad with low-calorie
   dressing
Coffee, decaffeinated coffee, or tea

DINNER: Spaghetti with Chicken Livers*
½ cup cooked string beans
½ Broiled Tomato*
½ cup unsweetened peaches
Coffee, decaffeinated coffee, or tea

DAY 7

BREAKFAST: ½ cup orange juice
½ cup Oatmeal with Raisins*
Coffee, decaffeinated coffee, or tea

LUNCH: Baked Rigatoni and Cheese*
½ cup cooked spinach
½ cup cooked sliced carrots
Coffee, decaffeinated coffee, or tea

DINNER: Linguini with Scallops*
Mixed green salad with low-calorie dressing
Wedge of honeydew melon
Coffee, decaffeinated coffee, or tea

DAY 8
BREAKFAST: ½ cup unsweetened pineapple juice
Ranch Omelet*
Coffee, decaffeinated coffee, or tea
LUNCH: Salad Taverna*
Mixed green salad with low-calorie dressing
Coffee, decaffeinated coffee, or tea
DINNER: Spinach Noodles with Veal and Pepper Sauce*
Pickled Cucumber Salad*
½ cup Lemon Ice*
Coffee, decaffeinated coffee, or tea

DAY 9
BREAKFAST: Cantaloupe Surprise*
Coffee, decaffeinated coffee, or tea
LUNCH: Broccoli–Noodle Soufflé*
Mixed green salad with low-calorie dressing
Coffee, decaffeinated coffee, or tea
DINNER: ½ cup chicken bouillon
Poached Chicken and Pineapple on Noodles*
½ cup cooked string beans
1 Sugar-free Lemon Cookie*
Coffee, decaffeinated coffee, or tea

DAY 10

BREAKFAST: ½ grapefruit
             Poached Egg on Raisin Toast*
             Coffee, decaffeinated coffee, or tea
LUNCH: Fettucini with Florentine Cheese Sauce*
             Mixed green salad with low-calorie dressing
             Coffee, decaffeinated coffee, or tea
DINNER: Buttermilk Dilled Flounder on Linguini*
             ½ cup cooked broccoli
             ½ Broiled Tomato*
             1 sugar-free baked apple
             Coffee, decaffeinated coffee, or tea

DAY 11

BREAKFAST: ½ cup orange juice
             ½ cup raisin bran cereal
             ½ banana, sliced
             ½ cup skim milk
             Coffee, decaffeinated coffee, or tea
LUNCH: Spinach Noodles with Broccoli–Pesto Sauce*
             Mixed green salad with tomato wedges and low-
                calorie dressing
             Coffee, decaffeinated coffee, or tea
DINNER: ½ cup tomato juice
             Chicken à la King on Macaroni*
             6 spears of cooked asparagus
             Prune Whip*
             Coffee, decaffeinated coffee, or tea

DAY 12

BREAKFAST: ½ cup apple juice
Cottage Cheese Omelet*
Coffee, decaffeinated coffee, or tea

LUNCH: Pasta Bow Ties with Yogurt–Mushroom Sauce*
½ cup cooked string beans
Coffee, decaffeinated coffee, or tea

DINNER: ½ cup bouillon
Shrimp Ratatouille on Noodles*
Green salad with low-calorie dressing
Sugar-free Chocolate Cookie*
Coffee, decaffeinated coffee, or tea

DAY 13

BREAKFAST: ½ cup unsweetened pineapple juice
2 shredded wheat biscuits with ½ sliced banana
½ cup skim milk
Coffee, decaffeinated coffee, or tea

LUNCH: Linguini with Stir-fry Zucchini Sauce*
Mixed green salad with grated carrot and low-calorie dressing
Coffee, decaffeinated coffee, or tea

DINNER: ½ cup tomato juice
Turkey Tetrazzini*
½ cup cooked spinach
½ cup water-packed fruit salad
Coffee, decaffeinated coffee, or tea

DAY 14

BREAKFAST:	½ sliced orange
	1 poached egg on whole wheat toast
	Coffee, decaffeinated coffee, or tea
LUNCH:	Tuna–Pasta Salad*
	Mixed green salad with low-calorie dressing
	Coffee, decaffeinated coffee, or tea
DINNER:	Linguini with Zucchini and Ham*
	½ cup cooked carrots
	Bisque Tortoni* (or ½ cup vanilla ice milk)
	Coffee, decaffeinated coffee, or tea

Five

Low-Calorie
Pasta Sauces

If pasta isn't "fattening," why does it have the reputation for being so? It's not the pasta itself that is high in calories, but it is often the sauce used with the pasta. Most restaurants and home cooks start a sauce with several tablespoons of olive oil or other fat, at 100 calories for each tablespoon of fat used. If a fatty ground meat is used for flavor and texture, that can add hundreds more calories to the sauce. On top of all of these calories, grated cheese may be sprinkled liberally over each serving without anyone realizing it adds up to 21 calories a level tablespoon.

Not all sauces for pasta are tomato-based meat sauces. Some gourmet chefs create masterpieces by using lots of butter and heavy cream before slathering the pasta with grated cheese. Take, for example, Fettucini Alfredo. A 5-ounce cooked portion of pasta at 210 calories can rapidly swell to 1,000 calories with such treatment. And you may swell with it!

This chapter of recipes will show you how to create very low-calorie sauces for the pasta you love. If you like creamy white sauced pasta, be sure to have a jar of the Fat-Free White Sauce Mix on hand (see recipe page 34) at a mere 52 calories per half cup serving.

When purchasing ground meat for the Mini-Meat Sauce, be sure that it is very lean or grind your own in a food processor. Note that a small amount of meat can go a long way to give you flavor and protein in your meal.

There will be times when you don't have the time or patience to create a sauce for the pasta and decide to use a commercial tomato-based product. Plain tomato sauce is 60 calories for an 8-ounce can, or 15 calories per ¼-cup serving. Meatless spaghetti sauce totals about 70 calories per ¼-cup serving. A 6-ounce can of tomato paste contains 136 calories, which can be cut down by adding onions, green peppers, mushrooms, and some water to make a larger quantity of sauce with fewer calories for each portion.

Fat will add the most calories to your pasta dishes, because it has twice the calories of protein and carbohydrates. Omit it wherever possible. Pay special attention to how it is done throughout this book. If you do use cheese, use the low-fat skim milk varieties. Measure the amount of grated Parmesan cheese you sprinkle over your pasta. Use plain low-fat yogurt instead of heavy cream or sour cream. If it is necessary to use oil to start a sauce, use a teaspoon or so in a nonstick frying pan and stir-fry the ingredients you are sautéing. Remember that the fat you don't eat will also be the fat you don't wear!

This chapter has low-calorie sauce recipes for pasta that will cook almost as quickly as the pasta itself. This is not only fast food, it is economical and nutritious as well.

MEATLESS SPAGHETTI SAUCE

1 35-ounce can Italian tomatoes in purée
1 6-ounce can tomato paste
1 onion, finely diced
½ teaspoon dried basil
½ teaspoon dried oregano

Put the tomatoes and tomato paste into a large saucepan. Add the onion, basil, and oregano. Cover and simmer over low heat for 30 minutes. Mash tomatoes into purée, using a slotted spoon or a potato masher. Use as a sauce for pasta.

Makes 5 cups of sauce. Each cup of sauce has 98 calories.

Note: The sauce may be prepared and refrigerated for 1 week. If desired, commercially prepared meatless spaghetti sauce may be used in its place.

BOLOGNESE SAUCE

4 ounces fresh mushrooms, sliced
1 onion, finely diced
1 garlic clove, minced
1 8-ounce can tomato sauce
¼ teaspoon honey
½ teaspoon dried basil
   Dash of freshly ground black pepper

Sauté the mushrooms, onion, and garlic in a nonstick frying pan, adding a tiny bit of water to make stirring easier. Let the water evaporate as the vegetables become limp. Add the tomato sauce, honey, basil, and pepper and cook for 5 minutes, stirring occasionally. Serve over pasta. *Makes 2 servings. Each serving has 58 calories.*

Note: The sauce will keep for 1 week in your refrigerator.

MINI-MEAT SAUCE

½ pound lean ground beef
1 onion, finely diced
1 garlic clove, finely minced
1 green bell pepper, finely diced
1 35-ounce can Italian tomatoes with basil
1 6-ounce can tomato paste

Crumble the ground beef and brown in large nonstick frying pan. Stir and break beef apart into tiny particles as it cooks. Add the onion, garlic, and green pepper. Cook and stir until the vegetables are limp. Add the tomatoes and tomato paste. Cover and cook for 25 minutes, breaking the tomatoes apart and mashing them as the sauce cooks.

Makes 6 cups of sauce. Each cup of sauce has 124 calories.

Note: Extra sauce may be refrigerated for up to 1 week or may be frozen for up to 2 months.

PESTO SAUCE

2 teaspoons olive oil
1 cup fresh basil leaves
¼ cup chopped fresh parsley leaves
2 garlic cloves, minced
2 tablespoons grated Parmesan cheese

Combine all the ingredients in the container of an electric blender and process until smooth.

Makes 2 servings. Each serving has 65 calories.

Note: This is a sauce that is high in fat. Use it only when you have had a low-fat intake with all other meals of the day. Serve on linguini or spaghetti, with cooked vegetables, such as zucchini, spinach, or broccoli on the side.

MARINARA SAUCE

- 1 **tablespoon olive oil**
- 1 **large onion, diced**
- 2 **garlic cloves, sliced**
- 1 **35-ounce can Italian tomatoes in purée**
- 1 **tablespoon chopped fresh parsley leaves**
- ½ **teaspoon dried oregano**
- ¼ **teaspoon freshly ground black pepper**

Heat the oil in a nonstick frying pan. Add the onion and garlic and sauté stirring frequently, until the onion is translucent. Add the tomatoes, parsley, oregano, and pepper. Simmer, covered, for 15 minutes. Press the mixture through a sieve to make a smooth sauce.

Makes 3 cups of sauce, or enough for 6 servings.
Each serving has 52 calories.

Note: The sauce may be refrigerated in a tightly covered container for up to 1 week. It may be frozen for up to 2 months.

TOMATO–YOGURT SAUCE

- 1 **garlic clove, minced**
- 3 **tablespoons tomato paste**
- ¼ **teaspoon dried oregano**
  Dash of freshly ground black pepper
- ½ **cup plain low-fat yogurt**

Sauté the garlic in a nonstick frying pan. Add the tomato paste, oregano, and pepper. Cook and stir until the sauce is hot. Remove from the heat and stir in the yogurt. Mix well. Reheat if necessary, but do not allow to boil. Use as a sauce for cooked pasta.

Makes 2 servings. Each serving has 45 calories.

FAT-FREE WHITE SAUCE MIX

2 cups nonfat dry powdered milk
¾ cup cornstarch
¼ cup chicken bouillon powder
4 teaspoons onion powder
1 teaspoon dried thyme
1 teaspoon dried basil
½ teaspoon freshly ground white pepper

Stir all the ingredients together in a medium-sized bowl. Store at room temperature in a tightly covered container. Makes 3 cups of mix. To reconstitute this mix, use ¼ cup of mix to 1 cup of liquid (such as skim milk or water) and add 1 tablespoon butter or margarine after the mixture has been stirred until it is smooth. Then heat and stir until thickened. Use as a white sauce for casseroles or sauces.

Makes 3 cups of mix. Each ¼ cup of mix makes enough for 2 servings.
Each serving has 50 calories.

CHEESE SAUCE

¼ cup Fat-Free White Sauce Mix (see preceding recipe)
1 cup water
¼ teaspoon dry mustard
¼ teaspoon paprika
2 ounces sharp Cheddar cheese, grated

Put the white sauce mix and water in a saucepan. Stir together until smooth. Add the mustard, paprika, and Cheddar cheese. Cook and stir over low heat until the cheese has melted.

Makes enough sauce for 2 servings. Each serving has 155 calories.

CREOLE SAUCE

1 **small onion, finely diced**
1 **garlic clove, finely diced**
1 **green bell pepper, finely diced**
2 **celery stalks, finely diced**
¼ **cup water**
1 **16-ounce can whole tomatoes**
1 **6-ounce can tomato paste**
1 **teaspoon chili powder**
⅛ **teaspoon black pepper**

Put the onion, garlic, green pepper, celery, and water in a large frying pan. Cover and simmer for 5 minutes. Add the tomatoes, tomato paste, chili powder, and pepper. Cover and simmer for 15 minutes longer.

Makes 2 cups of sauce, or enough for 4 servings.
Each serving has 145 calories.

Note: The sauce may be refrigerated for up to 1 week. Extra portions may be frozen for up to 2 months, if desired.

CLAM SAUCE

  1 **garlic clove, minced**
  1 **onion, finely diced**
 ½ **green bell pepper, finely diced**
  1 **cup chopped tomatoes**
 ½ **cup clam juice**
 ¼ **teaspoon dried oregano**
 ¼ **teaspoon dried thyme**
 ⅛ **teaspoon freshly ground black pepper**
  1 **cup chopped clams**

Combine the garlic, onion, green pepper, and chopped tomatoes in a saucepan. Add the clam juice, oregano, thyme, and pepper. Cover and simmer for 25 minutes. Add the chopped clams. Simmer, uncovered, 5 minutes longer.

Makes 2 servings. Each serving has 148 calories.

Note: The recipe may be halved to serve 1 or doubled to serve 4. Serve on cooked pasta.

Six

Meatless Pasta Entrées

Think of pasta as the main course for lunch. Have it with a simple vegetable sauce or with some low-fat cheese mixed through. Be sure to have a crisp mixed salad with low-calorie dressing or a low-calorie cooked vegetable on the side. Whenever possible, sprinkle a tablespoon (27 calories) of wheat germ into your salad. This adds the B-complex vitamins back into your diet—they are stripped from flour when it is refined and bleached.

If you have always had spaghetti with meat sauce or with meatballs, you're in for a change of pace with a variety of meatless sauces that will leave you well satisfied after the meal.

Don't let your meals get boring by using the same kind of pasta every time. There are so many choices, long, round, thin, flat, with holes, without holes, shells, bows, wheels, elbows, et cetera. Rigatoni and manicotti can be stuffed, lasagna noodles can encase a filling, while macaroni has lots of slurpy centers where sauce can hide. Let this be a time to have fun with pasta while you diet to lose that excess weight.

SPAGHETTI WITH
FRESH TOMATO–CUCUMBER SAUCE

    4 ounces spaghetti
1 ½ quarts boiling water
1 ½ cups coarsely chopped fresh tomatoes
   ¾ cup coarsely chopped peeled and seeded cucumber
   1 small garlic clove
   ¼ teaspoon dried oregano
   ⅛ teaspoon freshly ground black pepper

Gradually add the spaghetti to rapidly boiling water so that the water continues to boil. Cook, uncovered, stirring occasionally, until tender. Drain in a colander. Meanwhile, put half of the tomatoes and cucumber with the garlic, oregano, and pepper in a blender. Process until smooth. Add the remaining tomatoes and cucumber to the purée and pour over the cooked spaghetti.

Makes 2 servings. Each serving has 266 calories.

Note: The recipe may be halved to serve 1 or doubled to serve 4. Serve with hot cooked spinach on the side.

SPAGHETTI AND MUSHROOMS MARINARA

1 tablespoon olive oil
1 small onion, diced
1 garlic clove, minced
3 small ripe tomatoes, chopped
½ teaspoon dark brown sugar
¼ teaspoon dried thyme
⅛ teaspoon freshly ground black pepper
¼ pound fresh mushrooms, sliced
4 ounces spaghetti
1 ½ quarts boiling water

Heat the oil in a nonstick frying pan. Add the onion and garlic and sauté until the onion is translucent. Add the chopped tomatoes, brown sugar, thyme, pepper, and mushrooms. Cover and simmer over low heat for 15 minutes. Meanwhile, gradually add the spaghetti to rapidly boiling water so that the water continues to boil. Cook, uncovered, stirring occasionally, until tender. Drain in a colander. Serve the spaghetti topped with the sauce.

Makes 2 servings. Each serving has 360 calories.

Note: The recipe may be halved to serve 1 or doubled to serve 4. A crisp green salad, with sliced cucumbers and low-calorie dressing, completes the meal.

SPAGHETTI WITH BROCCOLI SAUCE

     4 ounces spaghetti
  1 ½ quarts boiling water
     1 cup broccoli flowerets
   ¼ cup evaporated skim milk
     1 tablespoon grated Parmesan cheese

Gradually add the spaghetti to rapidly boiling water so that the
water continues to boil. Cook, uncovered, stirring occasionally,
until tender. Drain in a colander. Chop the broccoli flowerets into
small pieces and add them to the spaghetti. Add the evaporated
milk and Parmesan cheese and toss. Serve at once.

Makes 2 servings. Each serving has 263 calories.

Note: The recipe may be halved to serve 1 or doubled to serve 4.
Serve with a mixed green salad with a low-calorie dressing.

FETTUCINI ALMOST-ALFREDO

     4 ounces fettucini
  1 ½ quarts boiling water
   ½ cup low-fat cottage cheese
     1 tablespoon grated Parmesan cheese
        Dash coarsely ground black pepper

Gradually add the fettucini to rapidly boiling water so that the water
continues to boil. Cook, uncovered, stirring occasionally, until
tender. Drain in a colander. Meanwhile, put the cottage cheese and
Parmesan cheese into an electric blender or food processor, and
blend into a smooth thin sauce. Toss the cooked drained fettucini
with the sauce. Sprinkle with coarse ground pepper and serve at
once.

Makes 2 servings. Each serving has 266 calories.

SPAGHETTI WITH CAULIFLOWER AND PEAS

  2 **cups cauliflower flowerets**
  ½ **cup fresh or frozen peas**
  ¼ **cup Fat-Free White Sauce Mix (see recipe page 34)**
  1 **cup water**
  ¼ **teaspoon Worcestershire sauce**
  1 **tablespoon grated Parmesan cheese**
  4 **ounces spaghetti**
1 ½ **quarts boiling water**

Cook the cauliflower and peas separately in boiling water until tender. Combine the white sauce mix with the 1 cup of water, Worcestershire sauce, and grated cheese. Cook over low heat, stirring constantly until thickened. Add the cooked cauliflower and peas to the sauce. Meanwhile, gradually add the spaghetti to rapidly boiling water so that the water continues to boil. Cook, uncovered, stirring occasionally, until tender. Drain in a colander. Toss with the sauce and serve.

Makes 2 servings. Each serving has 333 calories.

Note: The recipe may be halved to serve 1 or doubled to serve 4. Crisp romaine lettuce and sliced radishes with low-calorie dressing complete the meal.

SPAGHETTI WITH
EGGPLANT–MUSHROOM SAUCE

$\frac{1}{4}$ **pound fresh mushrooms, sliced**
  1 **small onion, finely diced**
  1 **small eggplant, peeled and diced**
  1 **8-ounce can tomato sauce**
$\frac{1}{4}$ **teaspoon dried oregano**
$\frac{1}{4}$ **teaspoon dried basil**
  4 **ounces spaghetti**
1 $\frac{1}{2}$ **quarts boiling water**

Put the mushrooms, onion, and eggplant in a large nonstick frying pan. Add the tomato sauce, oregano, and basil. Cover and simmer for 15 minutes, or until the vegetables are soft. Meanwhile, gradually add the spaghetti to rapidly boiling water so that the water continues to boil. Cook, uncovered, stirring occasionally, until tender. Drain in a colander and toss with the sauce.

Makes 2 servings. Each serving has 315 calories.

Note: The recipe may be halved to serve 1 or doubled to serve 4. Accompany with salad greens and grated raw carrot.

VEGETABLE–CHEESE–PASTA CASSEROLE

4 ounces spaghetti
1 ½ quarts boiling water
½ cup low-fat cottage cheese
½ cup plain low-fat yogurt
1 cup cooked cut string beans
1 cup cooked sliced carrots
¼ teaspoon dried dill
⅛ teaspoon freshly ground black pepper
¼ cup shredded Cheddar cheese

Gradually add the spaghetti to rapidly boiling water so that the water continues to boil. Cook, uncovered, stirring occasionally, until tender. Drain in a colander. Combine the cottage cheese and yogurt. Put half the spaghetti in a greased flat baking dish (a 9-inch square or a 1 ½-quart casserole dish) and top with half the cheese mixture. Make a layer of the beans and then the carrots. Sprinkle with dill and pepper. Spread with the remaining cheese mixture and top with the remaining spaghetti. Sprinkle the shredded Cheddar cheese over the spaghetti. Bake in a 350-degree oven for 25 minutes.

Makes 2 servings. Each serving has 370 calories.

Note: The recipe may be halved to serve 1 or doubled to serve 4. Flaked water-packed tuna may be added to the vegetable layer to make a complete meal.

FETTUCINI WITH ZUCCHINI SAUCE

1 **chicken bouillon cube**
¼ **cup boiling water**
½ **fresh zucchini, shredded**
3 **scallions, finely chopped**
¼ **cup fresh mushrooms, sliced**
4 **ounces fettucini**
1 ½ **quarts boiling water**
   Freshly ground black pepper

Melt the bouillon cube in the ¼ cup boiling water. Add the zucchini, scallions, and mushrooms and simmer until the vegetables are barely tender, but still crisp. Meanwhile, gradually add the fettucini to rapidly boiling water so that the water continues to boil. Cook, uncovered, stirring occasionally, until tender. Drain the fettucini in a colander and add it to zucchini mixture. Toss well. Transfer to a platter and sprinkle with the black pepper.

Makes 2 servings. Each serving has 235 calories.

Note: The recipe may be halved to serve 1 or doubled to serve 4. Serve with a mixed green salad with a low-calorie dressing.

LINGUINI FLORENTINE

  1 **small onion, finely diced**
  1 **garlic clove, minced**
  1 **cup fresh spinach, washed and chopped**
  1 **tablespoon chopped fresh parsley leaves**
  ¼ **cup dry white wine**
  ⅛ **teaspoon freshly ground black pepper**
  ⅛ **teaspoon ground nutmeg**
  4 **ounces linguini**
1 ½ **quarts boiling water**
  2 **tablespoons grated Parmesan cheese**

Sauté the onion and garlic in a nonstick frying pan, stirring frequently. Add the chopped spinach, parsley, wine, pepper, and nutmeg. Cover and simmer for 5 minutes. Meanwhile, gradually add the linguini to rapidly boiling water so that the water continues to boil. Cook, uncovered, stirring occasionally, until tender. Drain in a colander and toss with the spinach sauce. Serve topped with grated cheese.

Makes 2 servings. Each serving has 275 calories.

Note: The recipe may be halved to serve 1 or doubled to served 4. Serve with a lean broiled lamb chop and a crisp green salad with a low-calorie dressing.

FETTUCINI WITH FLORENTINE CHEESE SAUCE

    4 ounces fettucini
1 ½ quarts boiling water
  ½ cup part skim ricotta
    2 tablespoons grated Parmesan cheese
  ¼ cup plain yogurt
    1 cup washed fresh spinach leaves
    2 tablespoons chopped fresh parsley leaves
  ⅛ teaspoon freshly ground black pepper
  ⅛ teaspoon dried basil

Gradually add the fettucini to rapidly boiling water so that the water
continues to boil. Cook, uncovered, stirring occasionally, until
tender. Drain in a colander. Meanwhile, purée the ricotta, Parmesan cheese, yogurt, spinach, parsley, pepper, and basil in a blender
or food processor. Toss with the cooked fettucini and serve.

Makes 2 servings. Each serving has 308 calories.

Note: The recipe may be halved to serve 1 or doubled to serve 4.
Serve with a salad of romaine lettuce and grated carrot with a
low-calorie dressing.

LINGUINI WITH STIR-FRY ZUCCHINI SAUCE

  4 **ounces linguini**
1 ½ **quarts boiling water**
  1 **tablespoon olive oil**
  1 **garlic clove, minced**
  1 **cup thinly sliced zucchini**
  1 **cup diagonally sliced celery**
  ¼ **teaspoon dried basil**
  ⅛ **teaspoon freshly ground black pepper**
  ½ **cup cherry tomatoes**

Gradually add the linguini to rapidly boiling water so that the water continues to boil. Cook, uncovered, stirring occasionally, until tender. Drain in a colander. Meanwhile, heat the olive oil in a wok or nonstick frying pan. Add the garlic, zucchini, celery, basil, and pepper. Stir-fry for about 5 minutes, or until the vegetables are tender but still crisp. Add the tomatoes and cook for several minutes longer. Serve over cooked linguini.

Makes 2 servings. Each serving has 310 calories.

Note: The recipe may be halved to serve 1 or doubled to serve 4. Serve with a crisp green salad with a low-calorie dressing.

SPINACH NOODLES ROMAGNA

1 onion, finely diced
1 garlic clove
1 tablespoon olive oil
2 tablespoons chopped fresh parsley leaves
1 cup Meatless Spaghetti Sauce (see recipe page 31)
4 ounces spinach fettucini
1 ½ ounces boiling water

Heat the olive oil in a nonstick frying pan. Add the onion and garlic and sauté. Add the parsley and spaghetti sauce, cover and cook for 5 minutes. Meanwhile, gradually add the fettucini to rapidly boiling water so that the water continues to boil. Cook, uncovered, stirring occasionally, until tender. Drain in a colander. Toss with the sauce and serve.

Makes 2 servings. Each serving has 365 calories.

COTTAGE CHEESE–NOODLE OMELET

2 eggs
1 tablespoon cold water
¼ cup cooked fine egg noodles
¼ cup low-fat cottage cheese
1 tablespoon seedless golden raisins

Beat the eggs and water together. Add the cooked noodles and combine thoroughly. Pour into a nonstick frying pan. As the edges solidify, lift them to let the liquid egg run out to the edges. While still moist, turn the omelet out onto a plate. Combine the cottage cheese and raisins and spoon the mixture over half the omelet. Fold the omelet to cover the filling.

Makes 1 serving. Each serving has 271 calories.

SPINACH NOODLES WITH BROCCOLI–PESTO SAUCE

  4 ounces spinach fettucini
1 ½ quarts boiling water
  1 cup chopped fresh or frozen broccoli
  ½ teaspoon dried basil
  1 teaspoon olive oil
  1 garlic clove, minced

Gradually add the fettucini to rapidly boiling water so that the water continues to boil. Cook about 8 minutes, uncovered, stirring occasionally, until tender. Drain in a colander. Meanwhile, cook the broccoli in a nonstick frying pan in a very small amount of water until it is fork-tender. Drain. Add the basil, oil, and garlic and toss and stir over very low heat for several minutes. Add to the cooked, drained fettucini and toss lightly. Serve at once.

Makes 2 servings. Each serving has 237 calories.

Note: The recipe may be halved to serve 1 or doubled to serve 4. Serve with half a large broiled tomato, topped with a pinch of rosemary.

GREEN BEANS AND
GREEN NOODLES PARMESAN

  1 **package frozen French-cut green beans**
  1 **small onion, diced**
  1 **garlic clove, minced**
  1 **tablespoon chopped fresh parsley leaves**
 ¼ **teaspoon dried tarragon**
  1 **8-ounce can tomato sauce**
  4 **ounces spinach fettucini**
1 ½ **quarts boiling water**

Put the green beans, onion, garlic, parsley, and tarragon in a
saucepan. Add tomato sauce and cook, covered, until the beans are
tender, about 6 minutes. Meanwhile, gradually add the fettucini to
rapidly boiling water so that the water continues to boil. Cook,
uncovered, stirring occasionally, until tender. Drain in a colander.
Serve the noodles topped with the beans and sauce.

Makes 2 servings. Each serving has 300 calories.

Note: The recipe may be halved to serve 1 or doubled to serve 4.
Serve with cooked carrots on the side.

SALAD TAVERNA

    4 ounces spinach fettucini
1 ½ quarts boiling water
    1 tablespoon olive oil
    1 tablespoon fresh lemon juice
    ¼ teaspoon garlic powder
    ⅛ teaspoon Tabasco sauce
    ½ cup part skim ricotta
    1 tomato, coarsely chopped
    2 pitted black olives, sliced
    2 tablespoons chopped fresh parsley leaves

Gradually add the fettucini to rapidly boiling water so that the water continues to boil. Cook, uncovered, stirring occasionally, until tender. Drain in a colander and cool. Combine the oil, lemon juice, garlic powder, and Tabasco sauce and mix well. Add the fettucini, ricotta, tomato, olives, and parsley. Toss to coat evenly.

Makes 2 servings. Each serving has 335 calories.

Note: The recipe may be halved to serve 1 or doubled to serve 4. Serve on crisp romaine lettuce leaves.

STRAW AND GRASS PASTA COMBO

   1 teaspoon butter or margarine
 ¼ pound fresh mushrooms, sliced
 ½ cup fresh or frozen peas
   2 tablespoons part skim ricotta
   2 tablespoons skim milk
   1 tablespoon grated Parmesan cheese
   2 ounces fettucini
   2 ounces spinach fettucini
1 ½ quarts boiling water

Melt the butter in a nonstick frying pan. Add the mushrooms and sauté for 5 minutes. Add the peas, cover, and cook until they are tender. Remove the frying pan from the heat. Blend the ricotta, skim milk, and Parmesan cheese together. Add the mixture to the mushrooms and peas. Gradually add all the fettucini to rapidly boiling water so that the water continues to boil. Cook, uncovered, stirring occasionally, until tender. Drain in a colander. Toss with the sauce.

Makes 2 servings. Each serving has 303 calories.

Note: The recipe may be halved to serve 1 or doubled to serve 4. Serve with a mixed raw vegetable salad with a low-calorie dressing.

BAKED NOODLES NEAPOLITAN

    4 ounces broad egg noodles
1 ½ quarts boiling water
    1 8-ounce can tomato sauce
    ¼ teaspoon dried basil
    1 cup part skim ricotta
    1 tablespoon finely sliced scallion
    ⅛ teaspoon freshly ground black pepper
    2 tablespoons grated Parmesan cheese

Gradually add the broad egg noodles to rapidly boiling water so that the water continues to boil. Cook, uncovered, stirring occasionally, until tender. Drain in a colander. Combine the tomato sauce and basil and pour the mixture into the bottom of a flat baking dish (1 quart). Combine the noodles, ricotta, and scallions and spoon the mixture into sauce. Sprinkle with the pepper and grated cheese. Bake in a 350-degree oven for 25 minutes.

Makes 2 servings. Each serving has 365 calories.

Note: The recipe may be halved to serve 1 or doubled to serve 4. Accompany with cooked spinach and carrots.

COTTAGE CHEESE–NOODLE PUDDING

     8 **ounces broad egg noodles**
     3 **quarts boiling water**
     1 **cup low-fat cottage cheese**
     1 **cup low-fat plain yogurt**
     1 **egg**
     1 **teaspoon fresh lemon juice**
     1 **teaspoon vanilla extract**
    ½ **teaspoon ground cinnamon**

Gradually add the broad egg noodles to rapidly boiling water so
that the water continues to boil. Cook, uncovered, stirring occasionally, until tender. Drain in a colander. Combine the cottage
cheese, yogurt, and egg. Mix until smooth. Add the lemon juice,
vanilla, and cinnamon. Toss the mixture lightly through the noodles. Spoon into a greased flat baking dish (1½ quart). Bake in a
350-degree oven for 1 hour, or until lightly browned.

Makes 4 servings. Each serving has 311 calories.

Note: Serve with a fresh fruit salad. Extra portions may be refrigerated for up to 3 days or frozen for up to 2 months.

NOODLE OMELET

    4 ounces fine egg noodles
1 ½ quarts boiling water
    3 eggs
    1 tablespoon water
   ½ teaspoon celery seed
   ½ teaspoon dried parsley flakes
   ⅛ teaspoon freshly ground black pepper

Gradually add the fine egg noodles to rapidly boiling water so that the water continues to boil. Cook, uncovered, stirring occasionally, until tender. Drain in a colander. Beat the eggs, water, celery seed, parsley, and pepper together. Add the cooked noodles and mix well. Cook in a nonstick frying pan. Push the mixture aside as it cooks to permit the uncooked portions to flow to the bottom of the pan. When the omelet is completely set, fold in half and serve.

Makes 2 servings. Each serving has 323 calories.

Note: Use 1 jumbo egg and half the remaining ingredients to serve 1. Serve with a broiled tomato topped with a sprinkling of dried oregano.

BROCCOLI–NOODLE SOUFFLÉ

    4 ounces fine egg noodles
1 ½ quarts boiling water
    1 10-ounce package frozen chopped broccoli, thawed
    1 tablespoon grated onion
    ⅛ teaspoon ground nutmeg
    ⅛ teaspoon freshly ground black pepper
    2 tablespoons Fat-Free White Sauce Mix (see recipe page 34)
    ½ cup water
    3 eggs, separated

Gradually add the fine egg noodles to rapidly boiling water so that
the water continues to boil. Cook, uncovered, stirring occasionally,
until tender. Drain in a colander. Add to the thawed broccoli. Add
the grated onion, nutmeg, and pepper. Combine the white sauce
mix with ½ cup water in a small saucepan. Cook and stir over low
heat until the mixture is thickened. Remove from the heat and stir
in the slightly beaten egg yolks. Add broccoli–noodle mixture. Beat
egg whites until stiff peaks form. Fold into broccoli–noodle mixture. Spoon into an ungreased 1-quart soufflé dish. Bake in a pre-
heated 350-degree oven for 35 minutes, or until lightly browned.
Serve at once.

Makes 2 servings. Each serving has 394 calories.

BAKED MACARONI AND COTTAGE CHEESE

  4 ounces elbow macaroni
1 ½ quarts boiling water
  1 egg
  ½ cup skim milk
  ¾ cup low-fat cottage cheese
  ½ teaspoon Worcestershire sauce
  ⅓ cup chopped onion
  ⅓ cup chopped celery
  1 tablespoon chopped fresh parsley leaves

Gradually add the elbow macaroni to rapidly boiling water so that the water continues to boil. Cook, uncovered, stirring occasionally, until tender. Drain in a colander. Beat the egg and add the milk. Stir the mixture into the cottage cheese. Add the Worcestershire sauce, onion, celery, and parsley. Stir the mixture through the cooked macaroni. Pour into a greased casserole (1 quart) and bake in a 350-degree oven for 35 minutes, or until lightly browned.

Makes 2 servings. Each serving has 363 calories.

Note: The recipe may be doubled to serve 4. Extra portions may be refrigerated for up to 3 days or frozen for up to 2 months. Serve with cooked string beans and sliced beets.

STUFFED EGGPLANT

 1 medium-sized eggplant
 1 small onion, diced
 2 celery stalks, sliced
 ½ cup tomato juice
 ¼ teaspoon dried oregano
 1 cup cooked elbow macaroni
 1 tablespoon grated Parmesan cheese

Cut the eggplant in half and carefully scoop out the flesh, leaving the shells unbroken. Dice the scooped-out eggplant and put it in a saucepan with the onion, celery, tomato juice, and oregano. Simmer about 15 minutes, until tender. Remove from the heat and add the macaroni. Spoon the mixture into the eggplant shells. Top with a sprinkling of grated cheese. Put the filled shells into a baking pan and bake for 20 minutes in a 350-degree oven.

Makes 2 servings. Each serving has 200 calories.

Note: The recipe may be doubled to serve 4. Serve with a crisp mixed green salad with a low-calorie dressing.

BAKED MACARONI
WITH SPINACH AND CHEESE

4 ounces elbow macaroni
1 ½ quarts boiling water
1 cup Mini-Meat Sauce (see recipe page 32) or
    commercial product
½ 10-ounce package frozen chopped spinach, thawed
1 tablespoon grated onion
½ cup part skim ricotta
¼ teaspoon ground nutmeg
⅛ teaspoon freshly ground black pepper

Gradually add the elbow macaroni to rapidly boiling water so that the water continues to boil. Cook, uncovered, stirring occasionally, until tender. Drain in a colander. Spoon a layer of the sauce into a small greased baking dish. Then spoon half the macaroni over the bottom of the baking dish. Top with a mixture of spinach, onion, ricotta, nutmeg, and pepper. Spoon the remaining macaroni over the top and pour the remaining sauce over all. Bake in a 350-degree oven for 20 minutes, or until heated through.

Makes 2 servings. Each serving has 369 calories.

Note: The recipe may be halved to serve 1 or doubled to serve 4. Serve with a mixed green salad with a low-calorie dressing.

COLD MACARONI AND PEAS SALAD

       4 ounces elbow macaroni
    1 ½ quarts boiling water
       1 cup frozen peas, thawed
       2 tablespoons chopped chives
       1 teaspoon dried dill
       ½ cup plain low-fat yogurt
       1 tablespoon grated Parmesan cheese
       2 lettuce cups

Gradually add the elbow macaroni to rapidly boiling water so that the water continues to boil. Cook, uncovered, stirring occasionally, until tender. Drain in a colander. Rinse with cold water and drain again. Place in a large bowl. Add the peas, chives, and dill. Add the yogurt and mix very well. Chill until ready to serve. Spoon the salad into the lettuce cups and top with a sprinkling of grated Parmesan cheese.

Makes 2 servings. Each serving has 320 calories.

Note: The recipe may be halved to serve 1 or doubled to serve 4. Use as a main course for lunch and garnish each serving with cooked asparagus spears and a slice of unsweetened pineapple.

MACARONI–SLAW SALAD

    4 ounces elbow macaroni
1 ½ quarts boiling water
  ¾ cup thinly sliced carrots
  ¾ cup shredded green cabbage
  ½ cup plain low-fat yogurt
    1 small onion, finely diced
  ¼ teaspoon celery seed
    Dash of freshly ground black pepper

Gradually add the elbow macaroni to rapidly boiling water so that the water continues to boil. Cook, uncovered, stirring occasionally, until tender. Drain in a colander. Rinse with cold water and drain again. Put the macaroni in a large bowl. Add the carrots and cabbage. Stir together the yogurt, onion, celery seed, and pepper. Add to the macaroni mixture and toss well. Chill until ready to serve.

Makes 2 servings. Each serving has 297 calories.

Note: The recipe may be halved to serve 1 or doubled to serve 4. Use as a lunch dish by adding a garnish of tomato wedges.

ZITI WITH
MUSHROOM–PEPPER SAUCE

¼ **pound fresh mushrooms, sliced**
1 **green bell pepper, seeded and diced**
1 **cup Meatless Spaghetti sauce (see recipe page 31)**
4 **ounces ziti**
1 ½ **quarts boiling water**

Put the mushrooms and green pepper in a large frying pan. Add
the spaghetti sauce, cover, and cook for 15 minutes, or until the
vegetables are tender. Meanwhile, gradually add the ziti to rapidly
boiling water so that the water continues to boil. Cook, uncovered,
stirring occasionally, until tender. Drain in a colander and serve
with the sauce.

Makes 2 servings. Each serving has 282 calories.

Note: The recipe may be halved to serve 1 or doubled to serve 4.
Extra sauce may be refrigerated for up to 3 days. Serve with a mixed
raw vegetable salad.

RIGATONI WITH HOT CHILI SAUCE

1 onion, diced
½ teaspoon hot red pepper flakes
1 garlic clove, finely minced
½ teaspoon chili powder
1 8-ounce can tomato sauce
4 ounces rigatoni
1 ½ quarts boiling water
2 tablespoons grated Romano cheese
  Pinch of freshly ground black pepper

Sauté the onion, red pepper flakes, and garlic in a nonstick frying pan, stirring frequently, until the onion is limp. Add the chili powder and tomato sauce. Cover and simmer for 10 minutes. Meanwhile, gradually add the rigatoni to rapidly boiling water so that the water continues to boil. Cook, uncovered, stirring occasionally, until tender. Drain in a colander. Toss the rigatoni with the sauce. Serve topped with grated cheese and pepper.

Makes 2 servings. Each serving has 290 calories.

Note: The recipe may be halved to serve 1 or doubled to serve 4. Serve with a fresh green salad with a low-calorie dressing.

BAKED RIGATONI AND CHEESE

½ cup part skim ricotta
¼ cup diced part skim mozzarella
1 tablespoon grated Parmesan cheese
⅛ teaspoon freshly ground black pepper
4 ounces rigatoni
1 ½ quarts boiling water
1 cup Meatless Spaghetti Sauce (see recipe page 31)

Combine the ricotta, mozzarella, and Parmesan cheese. Add the pepper and set aside. Gradually add the rigatoni to rapidly boiling water so that the water continues to boil. Cook, uncovered, stirring occasionally, until tender. Drain in a colander. Spoon ½ cup of the sauce into a small flat baking dish. Top with half the cooked rigatoni. Spread half the remaining cheese mixture over the rigatoni. Make a layer of the remaining rigatoni and top it with the remaining sauce. Bake in a 350-degree oven for 20 minutes.

Makes 2 servings. Each serving has 372 calories.

Note: The recipe may be halved to serve 1 or doubled to serve 4. Serve with cooked spinach and carrots.

RICOTTA-STUFFED MANICOTTI

> **4** manicotti tubes
> **1 ½** quarts boiling water
> **½** cup part skim ricotta
> **2** tablespoons grated Parmesan cheese
> **1** 8-ounce can tomato sauce
> **½** teaspoon dried oregano
> **2** tablespoons Italian-style seasoned bread crumbs

Gradually add the manicotti to rapidly boiling water so that the water continues to boil. Cook, uncovered, stirring occasionally, until tender. Drain in a colander. Combine the ricotta and grated Parmesan cheese and stuff into the tubes with the mixture. Put the stuffed manicotti side by side in a flat baking dish. Pour the tomato sauce over all. Sprinkle with the oregano and bread crumbs. Bake in a 350-degree oven for 25 minutes.

Makes 2 servings. Each serving has 328 calories.

Note: The recipe may be halved to serve 1 or doubled to serve 4. Serve with a crisp green salad.

MANICOTTI WITH CHEESE-VEGETABLE STUFFING

    4 manicotti tubes
1 ½ quart boiling water
    ½ cup part skim ricotta
    1 egg white
    ⅛ teaspoon garlic powder
    ⅛ teaspoon dried basil
    ⅛ teaspoon ground nutmeg
    1 tablespoon chopped fresh parsley leaves
    2 tablespoons finely diced green bell pepper
    2 tablespoons peeled, finely diced cucumber
    1 cup Meatless Spaghetti Sauce (see recipe page 31)

Gradually add the manicotti to rapidly boiling water so that the water continues to boil. Cook uncovered, stirring occasionally, until tender. Drain in a colander. Combine the ricotta and egg white and mix well. Add the garlic powder, basil, nutmeg, parsley, green pepper, and cucumber. Stuff the mixture into the cooked manicotti tubes. Spoon a layer of spaghetti sauce over the bottom of a small baking dish. Put the stuffed tubes side by side over the sauce. Pour the remaining sauce over the manicotti. Bake in a 350-degree oven for 20 to 25 minutes.

Makes 2 servings. Each serving has 313 calories.

Note: The recipe may be halved to serve 1 or doubled to serve 4. Accompany with cooked spinach or turnip greens.

PASTA BOWS AND SWISS CHEESE

    4 ounces pasta bow ties
1 ½ quarts boiling water
    1 tablespoon grated Parmesan cheese
    ½ cup diced Swiss cheese
    ¼ cup Fat-Free White Sauce Mix (see recipe page 34)
    1 cup tomato juice
    ⅛ teaspoon ground nutmeg
      Dash of freshly ground black pepper
    2 tablespoons shredded part skim mozzarella

Gradually add the pasta bow ties to rapidly boiling water so that the water continues to boil. Cook, uncovered, stirring occasionally, until tender. Drain in a colander. Add the Parmesan cheese and Swiss cheese and toss well. Combine the white sauce mix with the tomato juice, nutmeg, and pepper in a saucepan. Cook and stir over low heat until thickened. Mix the sauce with the pasta and cheese mixture. Pour into a small greased baking dish. Top with the shredded mozzarella. Bake in a 350-degree oven for 25 minutes.

Makes 2 servings. Each serving has 427 calories.

Note: The recipe may be halved to serve 1 or doubled to serve 4. Serve with a fresh spinach salad with a low-calorie dressing.

PASTA BOW TIES WITH
YOGURT–MUSHROOM SAUCE

¼ pound fresh mushrooms, sliced
1 onion, diced
1 chicken bouillon cube
½ cup boiling water
¼ cup plain low-fat yogurt
⅛ teaspoon freshly ground black pepper
¼ teaspoon dried dill
4 ounces pasta bow ties
1½ quarts boiling water

Cook the mushrooms and onion in a nonstick frying pan for a few
minutes until they are limp. Stir frequently. Combine the bouillon
cube with ½ cup boiling water, stirring to dissolve the cube. Pour
the mixture into the pan with the vegetables and cook, uncovered,
until the liquid is reduced by half. Remove from the heat and stir in
the yogurt, pepper, and dill. Meanwhile, gradually add the pasta
bow ties to rapidly boiling water so that the water continues to boil.
Cook, uncovered, stirring occasionally, until tender. Drain in a
colander. Toss with the mushroom sauce and serve.

Makes 2 servings. Each serving has 263 calories.

Note: The recipe may be halved to serve 1 or doubled to serve 4.
Serve with a 3-ounce lean broiled beef patty and a fresh green salad
with a low-calorie dressing.

PASTA SHELLS WITH UNCOOKED TOMATO SAUCE

2 **very ripe tomatoes, peeled and chopped**
1 **garlic clove, minced**
1 **cup chopped fresh basil leaves**
1 **tablespoon olive oil**
⅛ **teaspoon freshly ground black pepper**
4 **ounces uncooked pasta shells**
1 ½ **quarts boiling water**

Combine the tomatoes, garlic, basil, olive oil, and pepper in a bowl. Let stand at room temperature for 1 hour. Gradually add the pasta shells to rapidly boiling water so that the water continues to boil. Cook, uncovered, stirring occasionally, until tender. Drain in a colander. Toss the uncooked sauce with the hot cooked pasta.

Makes 2 servings. Each serving has 300 calories.

Note: The recipe may be halved to serve 1 or doubled to serve 4. Serve with a mixed green salad with a low-calorie dressing.

COLD PASTA WITH YOGURT PRIMAVERA

  4 ounces pasta spirals
1 ½ quarts boiling water
  ½ cup fresh broccoli flowerets
  ½ cup fresh or thawed frozen peas
  1 red bell pepper, seeded and diced
  1 tomato, diced
  1 scallion, sliced
  1 teaspoon fresh lemon juice
  ½ teaspoon dried dill
  ¼ cup plain low-fat yogurt

Gradually add the pasta shells to rapidly boiling water so that the water continues to boil. Cook, uncovered, stirring occasionally, until tender. Drain in a colander. Meanwhile, cook the broccoli flowerets and peas in a small amount of water until they are just tender. Drain. Combine the pasta and all the vegetables. Mix the lemon juice, dill, and yogurt together. Toss with the pasta and chill until ready to serve.

Makes 2 servings. Each serving has 290 calories.

PASTA TWISTS WITH BROCCOLI SAUCE

1 onion, diced
1 garlic clove, minced
1 16-ounce can whole tomatoes
1 tablespoon chopped fresh parsley leaves
¼ teaspoon dried basil
⅛ teaspoon freshly ground black pepper
1 10-ounce package frozen chopped broccoli, thawed
4 ounces pasta twists
1½ quarts boiling water
2 tablespoons grated Parmesan cheese

Sauté the onion and garlic in a nonstick frying pan until the vegetables are limp. Stir frequently. Add the tomatoes, parsley, basil, and pepper. Cover and cook for 5 minutes. Add the thawed chopped broccoli, cover, and cook for 5 minutes longer. Meanwhile, gradually add the pasta twists to rapidly boiling water so that the water continues to boil. Cook, uncovered, stirring occasionally, until tender. Drain in a colander. Toss with the broccoli sauce, top with the grated Parmesan cheese, and serve.

Makes 2 servings. Each serving has 346 calories.

Note: The recipe may be halved to serve 1 or doubled to serve 4. Serve with a fresh green salad with grated fresh carrot and a low-calorie dressing.

EGGPLANT LASAGNE

1 **medium-sized eggplant, peeled and diced**
4 **ripe tomatoes, peeled and diced**
2 **celery stalks, sliced**
1 **small onion, diced**
1 **garlic clove, diced**
1 **tablespoon chopped fresh parsley leaves**
½ **teaspoon dried basil**
9 **lasagne noodles**
1 **quart boiling water**
½ **cup tomato juice**
¼ **cup finely diced part skim mozzarella**

Cook the eggplant, tomatoes, celery, onion, garlic, parsley, and basil in a nonstick frying pan, stirring frequently, for about 10 minutes. Meanwhile, gradually add the lasagne noodles to rapidly boiling water so that the water continues to boil. Cook, uncovered, stirring occasionally, until tender. Drain in a colander and rinse to keep the noodles separate. Place 3 noodles side by side in a greased 9- by 13-inch baking dish. Top with a layer of half the eggplant mixture, then another layer of 3 noodles, then another layer of the remaining eggplant mixture, and finally the last 3 noodles. Pour the tomato juice over all. Sprinkle with the diced mozzarella and bake in a 350-degree oven for 25 minutes.

Makes 4 servings. Each serving has 308 calories.

Note: Extra portions may be refrigerated for up to 3 days.

LASAGNE FLORENTINE

9 **lasagne noodles**
1 **quart boiling water**
1 **tablespoon vegetable oil**
½ **pound fresh mushrooms, sliced**
2 **medium-sized onions, finely diced**
2 **garlic cloves, finely minced**
1 **pound fresh spinach, washed, trimmed, and torn**
   into small pieces
2 **cups coarsely chopped fresh carrots**
1 **cup part skim ricotta**
1 **egg**
1 **8-ounce can tomato sauce**
3 **tablespoons grated Parmesan cheese.**

Gradually add the lasagne noodles to rapidly boiling water so that the water continues to boil. Cook, uncovered, stirring occasionally, until tender. Drain in a colander and rinse to keep separate. Heat the oil in a large saucepan. Add the mushrooms, onions, and garlic, and sauté, stirring to keep them from sticking. Add the spinach and carrots. Cook, stirring constantly, until the spinach is tender, 2 to 3 minutes. Combine the ricotta and egg and beat well. Then add to the spinach mixture. Pour a thin layer of tomato sauce over the bottom of a 9- by 13-inch baking dish. Arrange 3 lasagne noodles in a layer over the sauce. Spread half the spinach mixture in a thin layer over the noodles. Sprinkle with 1 tablespoon of the Parmesan cheese. Top with 3 more lasagne noodles, spread the remaining spinach mixture over the noodles, and sprinkle with 1 tablespoon of the Parmesan cheese. Arrange the remaining lasagne noodles over top. Pour the remaining tomato sauce over all. Sprinkle with remaining tablespoon of Parmesan cheese. Bake in a 375-degree oven for 25 minutes. Let stand for 10 to 15 minutes before cutting.

Makes 6 servings. Each serving has 252 calories.

Seven

Pasta Entrées
with Meat

Once a day you should have a meat, poultry, or fish sauce on your pasta or with it. The meat recipes in this chapter call for the lean cuts of meat and only small quantities of these. If you eat a larger portion than indicated, you'd better start walking it off at 100 calories a mile!

Notice that these meat recipes skip the usual step of sautéing some of the ingredients in oil. This is to keep the calories down, and it does not affect the flavor of the dish in any way. You may be surprised at how satisfied you feel when you have finished with a pasta-based main dish, a small portion of meat in the sauce, and low-calorie cooked vegetables or a salad with low-calorie dressing to round out your vitamin and mineral intake.

You should plan to have meat only two or three times a week, using poultry and fish sauces for the remainder of your meals. This will give you a nice variety of nutritional intake and help to keep the calorie counts within the goal of 1,000 a day.

A wide variety of herbs and spices are used to flavor the dishes in this chapter, making it possible to omit salt in recipes. Be sure to trim all meat of any visible fat before cooking.

SPAGHETTI WITH ONE MEATBALL

　1　**pound lean ground beef**
　1　**egg**
　1　**slice bread, soaked in water and squeezed dry**
　1　**tablespoon chopped fresh parsley leaves**
　2　**tablespoons grated onion**
　⅛　**teaspoon freshly ground black pepper**
　1　**35-ounce can whole tomatoes**
　1　**6-ounce can tomato paste**
　½　**teaspoon dried oregano**
　4　**ounces spaghetti**
1 ½　**quarts boiling water**

Combine the beef, egg, soaked bread, parsley, onion, and pepper and mix well. Form into 8 large meatballs. Put the tomatoes and tomato paste into a deep saucepan. Add the oregano and meatballs. Cover and cook for 20 minutes, or until the meatballs are cooked through. Gradually add the spaghetti to rapidly boiling water so that the water continues to boil. Cook, uncovered, stirring occasionally, until tender. Drain in a colander. Top each serving of spaghetti with 1 meatball and ½ cup of sauce.

Makes 2 servings, with leftover meatballs and sauce. Each serving has
379 calories.

Note: Nondieters may have extra meatballs. Leftovers may be refrigerated for up to 4 days or frozen for up to 3 months. Serve with a crisp green salad with a low-calorie dressing.

BEEF STROGANOFF ON BROAD NOODLES

⅓ pound thinly sliced lean sirloin steak
1 onion, thinly sliced
¼ pound mushrooms, sliced
⅛ teaspoon freshly ground black pepper
¼ cup water
½ cup plain low-fat yogurt
4 ounces broad egg noodles
1½ quarts boiling water

Sauté the beef strips in a nonstick frying pan. Push the beef aside and add onion and mushrooms. Stir occasionally to keep from sticking. Add the pepper and water and cook for several minutes. Remove from the heat and add the yogurt. Meanwhile, gradually add the broad egg noodles to rapidly boiling water so that the water continues to boil. Cook, uncovered, stirring occasionally, until tender. Drain in a colander. Serve the beef mixture over the noodles.

Makes 2 servings. Each serving has 475 calories.

Note: The recipe may be halved to serve 1 or doubled to serve 4. Serve with cooked carrots and peas.

SWEDISH MEATBALLS ON BROAD NOODLES

⅓ pound ground lean beef
⅓ pound ground veal
1 egg
½ cup unsalted mashed potatoes
1 tablespoon grated onion
¼ teaspoon freshly ground black pepper
¼ teaspoon ground nutmeg
⅛ teaspoon ground ginger
½ cup water
8 ounces broad egg noodles
3 quarts boiling water

Combine the ground beef and veal with the egg, mashed potatoes, onion, pepper, nutmeg, and ginger. Form into 1-inch balls. Brown in a nonstick frying pan, shaking the pan occasionally to brown on all sides. Add ½ cup water to the pan, cover, and cook over low heat for 10 minutes. Meanwhile, gradually add the broad egg noodles to rapidly boiling water so that the water continues to boil. Cook, uncovered, stirring occasionally, until tender. Drain in a colander. Serve the meatballs and gravy over noodles.

Makes 4 servings. Each serving has 421 calories.

Note: Extra servings of meatballs may be frozen and served at another time, if preferred. Serve with cooked asparagus on the side.

SUKIYAKI ON FINE NOODLES

⅓ pound boneless sirloin steak
2 teaspoons sesame oil
1 onion, thinly sliced
2 celery stalks, thinly sliced
¼ pound mushrooms, sliced
1 beef bouillon cube
½ cup boiling water
1 tablespoon soy sauce
1 tablespoon dry sherry
4 ounces fine egg noodles
1 ½ quarts boiling water

Trim the beef of all visible fat. Slice into very thin strips. (This is easier to do if the beef is partially frozen before slicing.) Heat the oil in a wok or frying pan; add the beef and stir-fry until it is browned on all sides. Add the onion, celery, and mushrooms and stir-fry until the vegetables are limp. Combine the bouillon cube with the ½ cup boiling water and add the mixture to the frying pan. Stir in the soy sauce and sherry. Cook for several minutes. Meanwhile, add the fine egg noodles to rapidly boiling water so that the water continues to boil. Cook, uncovered, stirring occasionally, until tender. Drain in a colander. Serve the Sukiyaki over the noodles.

Makes 2 servings. Each serving has 493 calories.

Note: The recipe may be halved to serve 1 or doubled to serve 4. If snow pea pods are available, add them during the cooking time.

MEAT-STUFFED MANICOTTI

    4 manicotti tubes
 1/4 pound lean ground beef
    1 small onion, finely diced
 1/4 teaspoon garlic powder
 1/4 teaspoon dried oregano
    1 slice whole grain bread
 1/2 cup cooked chopped spinach
    1 tablespoon chopped fresh parsley leaves
    1 tablespoon grated Parmesan cheese
    1 tablespoon cold water
    1 cup Meatless Spaghetti Sauce (see recipe page 31)

Gradually add the manicotti to rapidly boiling water so that the
water continues to boil. Cook, uncovered, stirring occasionally,
until tender. Drain in a colander. Combine the ground beef, onion,
garlic powder, and oregano. Soak the bread in water, squeeze it dry,
and crumble into the meat. Add the spinach, parsley, cheese, and
cold water and mix well. Stuff the mixture into the manicotti tubes.
Spoon half the sauce into a small baking dish. Arrange the stuffed
manicotti over the sauce; then top with the remaining sauce. Cover
with foil and bake in a 350-degree oven for 30 minutes.

Makes 2 servings. Each serving has 442 calories.

Note: The recipe may be halved to serve 1 or doubled to serve 4.
Extra portions may be refrigerated for up to 2 days or frozen for up
to 2 months. Serve with cooked carrots and a fresh green salad.

STUFFED BAKED MANICOTTI

    4 **manicotti tubes**
1 ½ **quarts boiling water**
  ½ **cup part skim ricotta**
  ¼ **cup shredded part skim mozzarella**
    1 **tablespoon grated Parmesan cheese**
    1 **cup Mini-Meat Sauce (see recipe page 32)**
    2 **tablespoons Italian-style seasoned bread crumbs**

Gradually add the manicotti to rapidly boiling water so that the water continues to boil. Cook, uncovered, stirring occasionally, until tender. Drain in a colander. Combine the ricotta and mozzarella and stuff noodle tubes with the mixture. Place the manicotti side by side in a small baking dish. Top with the Meat Sauce and sprinkle with the bread crumbs. Bake in a 350-degree oven for 30 minutes.

Makes 2 servings. Each serving has 375 calories.

Note: The recipe may be halved to serve 1 or doubled to serve 4. Serve with a crisp mixed green salad with a low-calorie dressing.

BEEF–NOODLE RAGOUT

⅓ pound lean ground beef
1 onion, diced
1 green bell pepper, diced
¼ pound mushrooms, sliced
1 zucchini, sliced
1 ½ cups tomato juice
1 cup fine egg noodles
1 bay leaf
¼ teaspoon dried thyme
⅛ teaspoon freshly ground black pepper

Brown the beef in a nonstick frying pan, breaking it into tiny particles as it browns. Add the onion, green pepper, mushrooms, and zucchini. Stir in the tomato juice, cover, and cook for 5 minutes. Then add noodles and cook, covered, for 5 minutes or longer, stirring frequently.

Makes 2 servings. Each serving has 395 calories.

Note: The recipe may be halved to serve 1 or doubled to serve 4. Serve with a fresh green salad, with sliced radishes, and a low-calorie dressing.

PENNE WITH
EGGPLANT–TOMATO MEAT SAUCE

  ¼ pound lean ground beef
  1 small eggplant, peeled and cubed
  1 onion, thinly sliced
  1 16-ounce can whole tomatoes
  1 tablespoon chopped fresh parsley leaves
  ¼ teaspoon dried basil
  ⅛ teaspoon freshly ground black pepper
  4 ounces penne (tubed pasta)
1 ½ quarts boiling water

Brown the beef in a nonstick frying pan, breaking it into tiny particles as it browns. Add the eggplant, onion, tomatoes, parsley, basil, and pepper. Cover and simmer for 15 minutes, or until the eggplant is tender. Gradually add the penne to rapidly boiling water so that the water continues to boil. Cook, uncovered, stirring occasionally, until tender. Drain in a colander. Combine the pasta with the eggplant sauce and serve.

Makes 2 servings. Each serving has 435 calories.

Note: The recipe can be halved to serve 1 or doubled to serve 4. Serve with a salad of romaine lettuce with a low-calorie dressing.

MINI MEATBALLS ON RIGATONI

⅓ pound lean ground beef
¼ cup Italian-style seasoned bread crumbs
1 egg white
1 tablespoon grated onion
1 tablespoon finely chopped fresh parsley
⅛ teaspoon freshly ground black pepper
1 8-ounce can tomato sauce
½ teaspoon dried oregano
4 ounces rigatoni
1½ quarts boiling water

Combine the ground beef, bread crumbs, egg white, onion, parsley, and pepper and mix well. Form into tiny meatballs and put them in a nonstick frying pan. Pour tomato sauce over all and sprinkle with the oregano. Cover and cook over low heat for 15 minutes. Meanwhile, gradually add the rigatoni to rapidly boiling water so that the water continues to boil. Cook, uncovered, stirring occasionally, until tender. Drain in a colander. Serve the rigatoni with meatballs and sauce.

Makes 2 servings. Each serving has 440 calories.

Note: The recipe may be halved to serve 1 or doubled to serve 4. Serve with cooked spinach.

SHISH KEBAB AND LINGUINI PESTO

    8 cubes (about ⅓ pound) lean boneless lamb
    1 green bell pepper, cut into chunks
    4 mushroom caps
    2 cherry tomatoes
    ¼ teaspoon dried thyme
    ⅛ teaspoon freshly ground black pepper
    4 ounces linguini
 1 ½ quarts boiling water
       Pesto Sauce (see recipe page 32)

Using 2 metal skewers, alternate the lamb cubes with the green pepper chunks, and mushroom caps. Put a cherry tomato on the end of each skewer. Season the kebabs with thyme and pepper. Broil for 5 minutes, turn, and broil until done. Meanwhile, gradually add the linguini to rapidly boiling water so that the water continues to boil. Cook, uncovered, stirring occasionally, until tender. Drain in a colander. Make the Pesto Sauce and toss with the linguini. Serve with the skewered meat and vegetables on the side.

Makes 2 servings. Each serving has 445 calories.

Note: The recipe may be halved to serve 1 or doubled to serve 4. Serve with a crisp green salad with a low-calorie dressing.

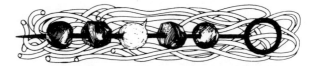

SPINACH NOODLES WITH VEAL AND PEPPER SAUCE

1 **garlic clove, minced**
1 **small onion, finely diced**
1 **green bell pepper, cubed**
1 **8-ounce can tomato sauce**
¼ **pound boneless veal, cut into tiny cubes**
¼ **teaspoon dried oregano**
⅛ **teaspoon freshly ground black pepper**
4 **ounces spinach fettucini**
1 ½ **quarts boiling water**

Sauté the garlic, onion, and green pepper in a nonstick frying pan for several minutes, stirring constantly. Add the tomato sauce, veal cubes, oregano, and pepper. Cover and simmer for 20 minutes, stirring constantly. Just before the veal is done, gradually add the fettucini to rapidly boiling water so that the water continues to boil. Cook, uncovered, stirring occasionally, until tender. Drain in a colander and serve with the veal sauce.

Makes 2 servings. Each serving has 363 calories.

Note: The recipe may be halved to serve 1 or doubled to serve 4. Serve with a crisp green salad with a low-calorie dressing.

FETTUCINI WITH ROSEMARY VEAL SAUCE

¼ pound boneless veal, cut into small cubes
1 onion, thinly sliced
1 garlic clove, finely minced
½ carrot, grated
1 8-ounce can tomato sauce
½ teaspoon dried rosemary
4 ounces fettucini
1 ½ quarts boiling water

Put the veal, onion, garlic, and carrot in a large frying pan. Add the tomato sauce and rosemary. Cover and simmer for 25 minutes, or until the meat is tender. Meanwhile, gradually add the fettucini to rapidly boiling water so that the water continues to boil. Cook, uncovered, stirring occasionally, until tender. Drain in a colander and serve with sauce.

Makes 2 servings. Each serving has 370 calories.

Note: The recipe may be halved to serve 1 or doubled to serve 4. Serve with a mixed green salad with a low-calorie dressing.

OSSO BUCO WITH PASTA BOW TIES

     2 slices (1 inch thick) veal shank with bone
     1 garlic clove, minced
     1 small onion, finely diced
     1 small carrot, grated
     1 tablespoon finely chopped fresh parsley
     1 teaspoon dried rosemary
     1 16-ounce can stewed tomatoes
     4 ounces pasta bow ties
  1 ½ quarts boiling water

Put the veal shank slices, garlic, onion, carrot, parsley, rosemary, and stewed tomatoes in a heavy frying pan. Cover and cook over low heat for 1 hour, or until the veal is tender. When ready to serve, gradually add the pasta bow ties to rapidly boiling water so that the water continues to boil. Cook, uncovered, stirring occasionally, until tender. Drain in a colander. Serve the veal and sauce over the pasta bows.

Makes 2 servings. Each serving has 430 calories.

Note: The recipe may be halved to serve 1 or doubled to serve 4. Serve with a mixed green salad with a low-calorie dressing.

MACARONI, HAM, AND FRUIT COMBO

    4 ounces elbow macaroni
1 ½ quarts boiling water
  ½ cup ham cut in strips
    1 orange, peeled and sectioned, seeds removed
    1 apple, diced
  ½ cup drained unsweetened pineapple tidbits
  ½ cup lemon low-fat yogurt
    2 crisp lettuce cups

Gradually add the elbow macaroni to rapidly boiling water so that
the water continues to boil. Cook, uncovered, stirring occasionally,
until tender. Drain in a colander. Combine the macaroni with the
ham, orange sections, diced apple, and pineapple tidbits. Toss
lightly with the lemon yogurt. Spoon into mounds in the lettuce
cups.

Makes 2 servings. Each serving has 470 calories.

Note: The recipe may be halved to serve 1 or doubled to serve 4.
Garnish with carrot and celery sticks.

LINGUINI WITH ZUCCHINI AND HAM

1   zucchini, sliced
1   garlic clove, finely minced
1   onion, diced
½   cup diced ham
¼   cup plain low-fat yogurt
4   ounces linguini
1 ½ quarts boiling water
⅛   teaspoon freshly ground black pepper
2   teaspoons grated Parmesan cheese

Cook the zucchini, garlic, and onion, in a nonstick frying pan for 5 minutes, stirring frequently. Add the ham and sauté with the vegetables until it is heated through. Remove from the heat and stir in the yogurt. Meanwhile, gradually add the linguini to rapidly boiling water so that the water continues to boil. Cook, uncovered, stirring occasionally, until tender. Drain in a colander. Toss the linguini with the zucchini sauce, top each with a pinch of pepper and a tablespoon of grated Parmesan cheese. Serve at once.

Makes 2 servings. Each serving has 393 calories.

Note: The recipe may be halved to serve 1 or doubled to serve 4. Serve with a fresh green salad with a low-calorie dressing.

CURRIED LAMB STEW
ON BROAD NOODLES

⅓ pound lean boneless lamb, cubed
1 small onion, diced
2 celery stalks, sliced
1 garlic clove, minced
¼ pound fresh mushrooms, sliced
2 tablespoons tomato paste
1 cup water
2 teaspoons curry powder
⅛ teaspoon freshly ground black pepper
4 ounces broad egg noodles
1 ½ quarts boiling water

Trim lamb to remove any visible fat. Sauté the onion, celery, garlic, and mushrooms in a large nonstick frying pan. Add the tomato paste, water, curry powder, and pepper and stir until smooth. Cover and simmer for 10 minutes. Add the lamb, cover, and simmer for 35 minutes, or until the lamb is tender. Gradually add the broad egg noodles to rapidly boiling water so that the water continues to boil. Cook, uncovered, stirring occasionally until tender. Drain in a colander. Serve the lamb and curry sauce over cooked noodles.

Makes 2 servings. Each serving has 405 calories.

Note: The recipe may be halved to serve 1 or doubled to serve 4. Serve with cooked zucchini on the side.

LIVER AND MUSHROOMS ON LINGUINI

½ pound sliced calf's liver
1 onion, thinly sliced
¼ pound fresh mushrooms, sliced
1 tablespoon chopped fresh parsley leaves
¼ cup dry white wine
4 ounces linguini
1 ½ quarts boiling water

Sauté the calf's liver in a nonstick frying pan. Add the onion, mushrooms, and parsley. Turn the liver and sauté all the ingredients for several minutes longer. Add the wine, cover, and cook over low heat until the liver is done. Meanwhile, gradually add the linguini to rapidly boiling water so that the water continues to boil. Cook, uncovered, stirring occasionally, until tender. Drain in a colander. Serve the liver and mushrooms over the cooked linguini.

Makes 2 servings. Each serving has 470 calories.

Note: The recipe may be halved to serve 1 or doubled to serve 4. Serve with cooked string beans.

LIVER STROGANOFF
ON PARSLEYED NOODLES

⅓   pound sliced calf's liver
¼   pound fresh mushrooms, sliced
1   small onion, sliced
¼   teaspoon dried thyme
    Dash of Tabasco sauce
¼   cup dry white wine
¼   cup plain low-fat yogurt
¼   teaspoon celery seed
4   ounces broad egg noodles
1 ½ quarts boiling water
1   tablespoon chopped fresh parsley leaves

Cut calf's liver into 1-inch strips. Sauté the liver strips in a nonstick frying pan, turning quickly with a spatula to brown all sides. Add the mushrooms, onion, thyme, and Tabasco sauce. Stir in the wine. Cover and simmer over low heat for several minutes, or until the liver is done. Add the yogurt and celery seed and remove the pan from the heat. Meanwhile, gradually add the broad egg noodles to rapidly boiling water so that the water continues to boil. Cook, uncovered, stirring occasionally, until tender. Drain in a colander. Add the fresh parsley to the noodles and toss to combine. Top with the liver mixture and serve at once.

Makes 2 servings. Each serving has 400 calories.

Note: The recipe may be halved to serve 1 or doubled to serve 4.

Eight

Pasta Entrées with Poultry

There are endless possibilities to be created when you combine pasta and poultry. The textures of both are highly compatible. It's a good idea to poach a chicken breast in a small amount of water, so that you always have some cooked chicken ready for dicing and adding to a pasta dish. The chicken will keep for several days in the refrigerator and you will be glad to have it available.

Poultry is equally delectable with a tomato sauce, a vegetable sauce, or a creamy sauce that has as its base yogurt or the Fat-Free White Sauce Mix on page 34. You will find that each nuance of flavor is different as you vary the pasta and the sauce. Here again, herbs and spices help to make every dish a taste experience.

Poultry is lower in calories than meat is, so slightly more generous portions are permitted. But the pasta is always the focal point, with the poultry as the auxiliary nutrient. Remember to plan a mixed green salad with low-calorie dressing, or a low-calorie cooked vegetable to accompany the main dish.

Instead of dreading a diet, you'll soon realize that you are in for an interesting and delicious adventure.

CHICKEN CACCIATORE ON LINGUINI

¼ pound mushrooms, sliced
½ green bell pepper, finely diced
1 onion, thinly sliced
1 garlic clove, minced
4 chicken thighs
1 cup peeled and chopped tomatoes
¼ teaspoon dried basil
¼ teaspoon dried oregano
⅛ teaspoon freshly ground black pepper
¼ cup dry red wine
4 ounces linguini
1½ quarts boiling water

In a nonstick frying pan, sauté the mushrooms, pepper, onion, and garlic until limp, stirring constantly. Add the chicken thighs, tomatoes, basil, oregano, pepper, and wine. Cover and cook over low heat for 35 minutes, or until the chicken is tender. Meanwhile, gradually add the linguini to rapidly boiling water so that the water continues to boil. Cook, uncovered, stirring occasionally, until tender. Drain in a colander. Serve the linguini topped with chicken and sauce.

Makes 2 servings. Each serving has 308 calories.

Note: The recipe may be halved to serve 1 or doubled to serve 4. Serve with a mixed green salad with a low-calorie dressing.

COQ AU VIN WITH NOODLES

     4 **broiler chicken thighs, skinned**
     1 **garlic clove**
   ¼ **pound fresh mushrooms, sliced**
     1 **small onion, sliced**
     1 **tomato, peeled and chopped**
   ½ **cup dry red wine, such as Burgundy**
   ½ **bay leaf**
   ¼ **teaspoon dried thyme**
     4 **ounces broad egg noodles**
1 ½ **quarts boiling water**

Brown the chicken thighs in a nonstick frying pan, turning them frequently. Push the chicken aside and add the garlic, mushrooms, and onion. Sauté until the onion is translucent. Add the tomato, wine, bay leaf, and thyme. Cover and cook for 25 minutes, or until the chicken is tender. Gradually add the broad egg noodles to rapidly boiling water so that the water continues to boil. Cook, uncovered, stirring occasionally, until tender. Drain in a colander. Serve the Coq au Vin on top of the noodles.

Makes 2 servings. Each serving has 494 calories.

Note: The recipe may be halved to serve 1 or doubled to serve 4. Serve with cooked broccoli.

DILLED CHICKEN AND NOODLES

    3 cups chicken broth
    2 cups cooked chicken chunks
    2 sprigs fresh dill
  ½ cup frozen peas
    2 ounces medium egg noodles
    Dash of freshly ground black pepper

Bring the chicken broth to a boil. Add the remaining ingredients and cook for 8 minutes. Serve in soup bowls.

Makes 2 servings. Each serving has 367 calories.

Note: Serve with a mixed raw vegetable salad with a low-calorie dressing.

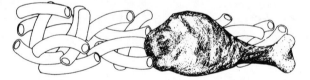

CHICKEN PAPRIKASH
ON BROAD EGG NOODLES

    4 **chicken thighs, skinned**
    1 **teaspoon sweet paprika**
  ¹/₈ **teaspoon freshly ground black pepper**
  ¹/₄ **cup water**
    1 **small onion**
  ¹/₄ **cup plain low-fat yogurt**
    4 **ounces broad egg noodles**
1 ¹/₂ **quarts boiling water**

Season chicken thighs with ¹/₄ teaspoon of the paprika and sprinkle them with the pepper. Broil 5 minutes on each side. Put the water and onion in a small frying pan and simmer until the onion is soft. Add the broiled chicken thighs to the frying pan and simmer until the water has almost evaporated and the chicken is tender. Stir the remaining paprika into the yogurt and pour the mixture over the chicken. Heat just through. Meanwhile, gradually add the broad egg noodles to rapidly boiling water so that the water continues to boil. Cook, uncovered, stirring occasionally, until tender. Drain in a colander. Serve the chicken and sauce over cooked noodles.

Makes 2 servings. Each serving has 482 calories.

Note: The recipe may be halved to serve 1 or doubled to serve 4.

POACHED CHICKEN AND PINEAPPLE ON NOODLES

    2 chicken breast halves, skinned and boned
    1 8-ounce can pineapple chunks packed in unsweetened juice
    1 teaspoon fresh lemon juice
    1 teaspoon dark brown sugar
    1 teaspoon soy sauce
  ¼ teaspoon ground ginger
    4 ounces fine egg noodles
1 ½ quarts boiling water

Put the chicken breast halves in a frying pan. Add the juice drained from the pineapple. Cover and cook over low heat for 15 minutes, or until the chicken is cooked through. Remove the chicken and add the lemon juice, brown sugar, soy sauce, and ginger to the pan. Cook and stir until smooth and hot. Add the pineapple chunks and chicken to the sauce. Gradually add the fine egg noodles to rapidly boiling water so that the water continues to boil. Cook, uncovered, stirring occasionally, until tender. Drain in a colander. Serve the pineapple, chicken, and sauce over the noodles.

Makes 2 servings. Each serving has 430 calories.

Note: The recipe may be halved to serve 1 or doubled to serve 4. Serve with cooked broccoli.

CHICKEN AND BEAN SPROUTS ON BROAD EGG NOODLES

    2 chicken breast halves, skinned and boned
    1 onion, sliced
    2 celery stalks, sliced
    1 cup bean sprouts
    1 chicken bouillon cube
  ½ cup boiling water
  ½ teaspoon dried dill
  ⅛ teaspoon freshly ground black pepper
    4 ounces broad egg noodles
1 ½ quarts boiling water
    1 teaspoon cornstarch

Cut the raw boneless chicken into large chunks. Put the chicken cubes in a frying pan with the onion, celery, bean sprouts, and bouillon cube mixed with ½ cup boiling water. Add the dill and pepper. Cover and simmer over low heat for 15 minutes, or until the chicken is tender. Meanwhile, gradually add the broad egg noodles to rapidly boiling water so that the water continues to boil. Cook, uncovered, stirring occasionally, until tender. Drain in a colander. Combine the cornstarch with just enough cold water to make a thin paste. Stir the paste into the chicken mixture and heat to thicken. Serve the chicken over the cooked noodles.

Makes 2 servings. Each serving has 420 calories.

Note: The recipe may be halved to serve 1 or doubled to serve 4. Serve with cooked asparagus or broccoli.

NOODLES WITH CHICKEN–BROCCOLI SAUCE

    1 **cup cooked chicken, diced**
    2 **teaspoons peanut oil or other vegetable oil**
  ¼ **pound mushrooms, sliced**
    3 **scallions, sliced thin**
    1 **garlic clove, minced**
  ¼ **teaspoon ground ginger**
    2 **teaspoons soy sauce**
    1 **10-ounce package frozen chopped broccoli, thawed**
    4 **ounces medium egg noodles**
1 ½ **quarts boiling water**

Sauté the diced chicken in the oil in a wok or a nonstick frying pan. Add the mushrooms, scallions, garlic, and ginger. Sauté while turning the ingredients frequently. Add the soy sauce and thawed chopped broccoli, cooking and turning until the broccoli is hot and tender, about 4 minutes. Gradually add the medium egg noodles to rapidly boiling water so that the water continues to boil. Cook, uncovered, stirring occasionally, until tender. Drain in a colander. Top each serving of noodles with the chicken–broccoli sauce.

Makes 2 servings. Each serving has 427 calories.

Note: The recipe may be halved to serve 1 or doubled to serve 4. Serve with hot cooked sliced carrots.

CHICKEN AND BROCCOLI TETRAZZINI

1 10-ounce package frozen chopped broccoli
4 ounces linguini
1 ½ quarts boiling water
1 cup cooked diced chicken
¼ cup Fat-Free White Sauce Mix (see recipe page 34)
1 cup skim milk
1 tablespoon grated Parmesan cheese

Cook the broccoli in boiling water until it is tender. Drain. Gradually add the linguini to rapidly boiling water so that the water continues to boil. Cook, uncovered, stirring occasionally, until tender. Drain in a colander. Combine the broccoli, linguini, and cooked chicken. Combine the white sauce mix and skim milk in a saucepan and mix until smooth. Cook over low heat until thickened. Add the grated Parmesan cheese. Pour the sauce into the linguini mixture and mix through. Pour into a greased 1 ½-quart baking dish and bake in a 350-degree oven for 25 minutes.

Makes 2 servings. Each serving has 475 calories.

Note: The recipe may be halved to serve 1 or doubled to serve 4. Serve with a mixed green salad with a low-calorie dressing.

CHICKEN STROGANOFF
ON BROAD EGG NOODLES

1 **whole chicken breast, skinned, boned, and halved**
1 **tablespoon fresh lemon juice**
1 **teaspoon butter**
¼ **teaspoon paprika**
¼ **cup dry white wine**
4 **ounces broad egg noodles**
¼ **cup plain low-fat yogurt**
1 ½ **quarts boiling water**

Sprinkle the chicken breast halves with the lemon juice. Melt the butter in a nonstick frying pan. Add the chicken and brown on all sides. Sprinkle with the paprika. Add the wine, cover, and cook over low heat for 25 minutes, or until the chicken is tender. Gradually add the broad egg noodles to rapidly boiling water so that the water continues to boil. Cook, uncovered, stirring occasionally, until tender. Drain in a colander. Put a portion of the noodles on each of two plates; top with a piece of cooked chicken. Add the yogurt to the cooking liquid in the frying pan. Mix well and reheat but not to the boiling point. Pour the sauce over the chicken and noodles and serve at once.

Makes 2 servings. Each serving has 402 calories.

Note: The recipe may be halved to serve 1 or doubled to serve 4. Serve with cooked carrots and a crisp green salad with a low-calorie dressing.

BAKED CHICKEN, CAULIFLOWER, AND RIGATONI

      4 ounces rigatoni
 1 ½ quarts boiling water
      1 small head cauliflower
      1 16-ounce can whole tomatoes
      1 cup diced cooked chicken
      1 tablespoon chopped fresh parsley leaves
      1 garlic clove, minced
      1 small onion, diced
    ⅛ teaspoon freshly ground black pepper

Gradually add the rigatoni to rapidly boiling water so that the water continues to boil. Cook, uncovered, stirring occasionally, until tender. Drain in a colander. Wash the cauliflower and break it into small pieces; add to rigatoni with the tomatoes, chicken, parsley, garlic, onion, and pepper. Spoon into a greased 1 ½-quart baking dish and bake in a 350-degree oven for 35 minutes, or until lightly browned.

Makes 2 servings. Each serving has 419 calories.

Note: The amount of rigatoni and chicken may be doubled and added to this list of ingredients to serve 4, using a medium-sized cauliflower.

OVEN-BAKED CHICKEN WITH SPIRALS MARINARA

¼ cup corn flake crumbs
¼ teaspoon paprika
⅛ teaspoon freshly ground black pepper
4 chicken thighs or 2 chicken breast halves, skinned
¼ cup skim milk
2 ounces pasta spirals
1 quart boiling water
½ cup Marinara Sauce (see recipe page 33) or commercial product

Combine the corn flake crumbs, paprika, and pepper. Dip the chicken parts into the skim milk and then into crumb mixture, coating them well. Place in a baking dish and bake in a 350-degree oven for 50 minutes, or until the chicken is tender. Meanwhile, gradually add the pasta spirals to rapidly boiling water so that the water continues to boil. Cook, uncovered, stirring occasionally, until tender. Drain in a colander. Toss with the Marinara Sauce and top with the crisp chicken.

Makes 2 servings. Each serving has 428 calories.

Note: The recipe may be halved to serve 1 or doubled to serve 4.

ZITI AND CHICKEN SALAD

    4 ounces ziti
1 ½ quarts boiling water
    1 cup diced cooked chicken
    ½ cup diced celery
    ½ cup diced cucumber, peeled and seeded
    ½ cup frozen peas, thawed
    ¼ cup plain low-fat yogurt
    1 tablespoon mayonnaise
    ¼ teaspoon dried dill

Gradually add the ziti to rapidly boiling water so that the water continues to boil. Cook, uncovered, stirring occasionally, until tender. Drain in a colander, rinse with cold water, and drain again. Combine the ziti with chicken, celery, cucumber, and peas. Mix together the yogurt, mayonnaise, and dill. Add to the ziti salad and toss to coat well. Chill until ready to serve.

Makes 2 servings. Each serving has 424 calories.

Note: The recipe may be halved to serve 1 or doubled to serve 4. Serve on a bed of lettuce and garnish with tomato wedges.

MACARONI–CHICKEN STUFFED PEPPERS

2 **large green bell peppers**
1 **tablespoon finely diced onion**
½ **cup diced cooked chicken**
1 **cup cooked elbow macaroni**
½ **teaspoon chopped fresh parsley leaves**
1 **tomato, peeled and chopped**
1 **egg, slightly beaten**
½ **cup tomato juice**
1 **tablespoon grated Parmesan cheese**

Cut green peppers in half lengthwise and remove the seeds. Combine the onion, chicken, macaroni, parsley, and chopped tomato. Add the beaten egg and mix thoroughly. Spoon the mixture into pepper cups. Arrange the peppers, stuffing side up, in a small baking dish. Pour the tomato juice around the peppers. Sprinkle the grated Parmesan cheese on top of the peppers. Bake in a 350-degree oven for 25 minutes.

Makes 2 servings. Each serving has 276 calories.

Note: The recipe may be halved to serve 1 or doubled to serve 4. Serve with a crisp green salad with grated carrot and a low-calorie dressing.

CHICKEN À LA KING ON MACARONI

         1 **chicken bouillon cube**
    ½ **cup boiling water**
    ¼ **pound fresh mushrooms, sliced**
         1 **small green bell pepper, diced**
         1 **pimiento, diced**
    ½ **cup fresh or frozen peas**
         1 **cup cubed cooked chicken**
         1 **tablespoon dry sherry**
         2 **teaspoons cornstarch**
    ⅛ **teaspoon freshly ground black pepper**
         4 **ounces elbow macaroni**
1 ½ **quarts boiling water**

Put the bouillon cube and the ½ cup boiling water in a saucepan and stir to dissolve the cube. Add the mushrooms, green pepper, pimiento, peas, and chicken. Cook for 5 minutes. Combine the sherry and cornstarch until smooth. Add to the saucepan and stir until the mixture thickens. Add the black pepper. Meanwhile, gradually add the elbow macaroni to rapidly boiling water so that the water continues to boil. Cook, uncovered, stirring occasionally, until tender. Drain in a colander. Serve the chicken and sauce on macaroni.

Makes 2 servings. Each serving has 396 calories.

Note: The recipe may be halved to serve 1 or doubled to serve 4. Serve with a crisp green salad with a low-calorie dressing.

ORIENTAL PASTA SALAD

    4 ounces pasta bow ties
1 ½ quarts boiling water
    2 ounces fresh snow peas, washed and trimmed
    1 red bell pepper, seeded and cut into strips
    2 scallions, sliced thin
1 ½ cups fresh broccoli flowerets and thinly sliced stems
    1 cup cooked diced chicken
    1 tablespoon peanut oil
    1 tablespoon red wine vinegar
  ¼ teaspoon Tabasco sauce
    1 teaspoon honey
  ¼ teaspoon garlic powder
  ¼ teaspoon ground ginger

Gradually add the pasta bow ties to rapidly boiling water so that the water continues to boil. Cook, uncovered, stirring occasionally, until tender. Drain in a colander and cool. Add the snow peas, red pepper, scallions, broccoli, and diced chicken. Combine peanut oil, vinegar, Tabasco, honey, garlic powder, and ginger and pour the dressing over the pasta mixture. Toss lightly. Cover and chill.

Makes 2 servings. Each serving has 449 calories.

Note: The recipe may be halved to serve 1 or doubled to serve 4. Diced turkey or water-packed tuna may be substituted for the cooked chicken.

SPAGHETTI MILANESE

1	tablespoon olive oil
1	small onion, finely diced
½	cup sliced fresh mushrooms
1	garlic clove, minced
4	chicken livers
¼	teaspoon dried oregano
¼	teaspoon dried basil
2	tomatoes, peeled and chopped
½	cup tomato juice
4	ounces spaghetti
1 ½	quarts boiling water

Heat the oil in a nonstick frying pan. Add the onion, mushrooms, and garlic and sauté for several minutes, stirring frequently. Cut the chicken livers into small chunks, add them to the skillet, and brown on all sides. Stir constantly to prevent sticking. Add the oregano, basil, chopped tomatoes, and tomato juice. Simmer for 15 minutes over low heat. Gradually add the spaghetti to rapidly boiling water so that the water continues to boil. Cook, uncovered, stirring occasionally, until tender. Drain in a colander. Serve with the sauce.

Makes 2 servings. Each serving has 424 calories.

Note: The recipe may be halved to serve 1 or doubled to serve 4. Serve with cooked spinach on the side.

SPAGHETTI WITH CHICKEN LIVERS

  1 onion, finely diced
  ½ pound chicken livers, cut in half
  ¼ pound fresh mushrooms, sliced
  ¼ cup water
  1 8-ounce can tomato sauce
  ¼ teaspoon dried thyme
  ⅛ teaspoon freshly ground pepper
  4 ounces spaghetti
1 ½ quarts boiling water

Put the onion, chicken livers, and mushrooms in a frying pan. Add ¼ cup water. Cover and simmer until the livers are tender. Add the tomato sauce, thyme, and pepper, cover, and heat through. Gradually add the spaghetti to rapidly boiling water so that the water continues to boil. Cook, uncovered, stirring occasionally, until tender. Drain in a colander. Serve the spaghetti topped with the livers and sauce.

Makes 2 servings. Each serving has 463 calories.

Note: The recipe may be halved to serve 1 or doubled to serve 4. Serve with cooked asparagus or string beans.

CHICKEN LIVERS HAWAIIAN

½ pound chicken livers, halved
1 green bell pepper, seeded and sliced
1 onion, thinly sliced
½ cup canned unsweetened crushed pineapple with juice
1 teaspoon soy sauce
¼ teaspoon dry mustard
¼ teaspoon ground ginger
4 ounces fettucini
1½ quarts boiling water

Cook the chicken livers, green pepper, and onion in a nonstick frying pan for 10 minutes, stirring frequently. Add the pineapple, soy sauce, mustard, and ginger and stir well. Meanwhile, gradually add the fettucini to rapidly boiling water so that the water continues to boil. Cook, uncovered, stirring occasionally, until tender. Drain in a colander. Serve with the chicken liver–pineapple sauce.

Makes 2 servings. Each serving has 459 calories.

Note: The recipe may be halved to serve 1 or doubled to serve 4. Serve cooked carrots and broccoli on the side.

TURKEY AND MACARONI SALAD

    4 ounces elbow macaroni
1 ½ quarts boiling water
    1 cup cubed cooked turkey
    ¼ cup frozen peas, thawed but not cooked
    1 carrot, finely diced
    2 celery stalks, finely diced
    1 tablespoon finely diced onion
    ½ cup plain low-fat yogurt
    1 teaspoon grated lemon rind
    ½ teaspoon dried dill

Gradually add the elbow macaroni to rapidly boiling water so that the water continues to boil. Cook, uncovered, stirring occasionally, until tender. Drain in a colander. Combine the macaroni with the turkey, peas, carrot, celery, and onion. Stir together the yogurt, grated rind, and dill. Combine thoroughly with the turkey salad.

Makes 2 servings. Each serving has 408 calories.

Note: The recipe may be halved to serve 1 or doubled to serve 4. Mound the salad on a bed of lettuce. Surround each serving with tomato wedges and a slice of unsweetened pineapple.

TURKEY TETRAZZINI

   4 ounces spaghetti
1 ½ quarts boiling water
  ¼ cup Fat-Free White Sauce Mix (see recipe page 34)
   1 cup chicken broth
  ½ cup sliced fresh mushrooms
  ¼ teaspoon Worcestershire sauce
   1 cup cooked diced turkey
   1 tablespoon grated Parmesan cheese

Gradually add the spaghetti to rapidly boiling water so that the water continues to boil. Cook, uncovered, stirring occasionally, until tender. Drain in a colander. Meanwhile, combine the white sauce mix with the broth in the saucepan. Add the mushrooms and Worcestershire sauce. Cover and cook for 3 minutes. Add the diced turkey and the cooked spaghetti. Pour the mixture into a greased 1-quart casserole. Top with the grated cheese. Bake in a 350-degree oven for 25 minutes.

Makes 2 servings. Each serving has 366 calories.

Note: The recipe may be halved to serve 1 or doubled to serve 4. Extra portions may be refrigerated for up to 3 days, or frozen for up to 2 months. Serve with cooked spinach and carrots.

Nine

Pasta Entrées
with Seafood

By now you must realize that fat in any form is the culprit that caused your excess padding. Fish has very little fat and that is why it's an ideal protein choice for a pasta sauce. The problem is that many people don't know how to cook fish without frying it. You can broil it, bake it, or poach it in a skillet with a small amount of liquid. The trick is to cook the fish just before eating it, and only as long as it takes to firm up the flesh and get it to the opaque stage. Overcooked fish can be tough and tasteless.

There are only a few kinds of meat, a few kinds of poultry, but endless varieties of fish to be explored and enjoyed. While it's wonderful to eat freshly cooked fish, there will be times when you'll be glad to have water-packed tuna on hand. There is such a difference in taste between white and light meat tuna that it is worth the extra money to purchase the white meat tuna in solid or chunk form. Be sure that you buy only the water-packed tuna—the oil-packed has roughly double the calories of the water-packed.

Fresh fish is really best, but other canned fish that are nicely combined with sauce for pasta are clams, crabmeat, oysters, and salmon. Don't forget to augment each fish and pasta dish with a serving or two of low-calorie vegetables. The object of a sensible diet is to have balanced nutritional intake while you take off excess weight!

FISH CREOLE ON FINE NOODLES

    1 onion, sliced
    1 green bell pepper, diced
    1 celery stalk, sliced
    1 16-ounce can whole tomatoes
   ¼ teaspoon dried thyme
   ⅛ teaspoon freshly ground black pepper
    2 slices (about ½ pound) cod or haddock fillets
    4 ounces fine egg noodles
 1 ½ quarts boiling water

Put the onion, green pepper, celery, tomatoes, thyme, and pepper in a nonstick frying pan. Cover and simmer for 10 minutes. Add the fish fillets, cover, and cook for 5 to 7 minutes, or until the fish flakes easily. Meanwhile, gradually add the fine egg noodles to rapidly boiling water so that the water continues to boil. Cook, uncovered, stirring occasionally, until tender. Drain in a colander. Serve the fish and sauce over the noodles.

Makes 2 servings. Each serving has 443 calories.

Note: The recipe may be halved to serve 1 or doubled to serve 4. Serve with a mixed green salad with a low-calorie dressing.

NOODLES AND SOLE AMANDINE

  2 **sole fillets (about ½ pound)**
 ¼ **cup fresh lemon juice**
 ¼ **cup dry white wine**
  1 **tablespoon chopped fresh parsley leaves**
  4 **ounces medium egg noodles**
  1 **tablespoon sliced almonds**
  1 **teaspoon butter**
1½ **quarts boiling water**

Arrange the fish in a nonstick frying pan. Pour the lemon juice over fish and marinate for 10 minutes before cooking. Add the white wine and parsley, to the pan. Cover and poach for 5 to 7 minutes, or until the fish flakes easily. Meanwhile, gradually add the medium egg noodles to rapidly boiling water so that the water continues to boil. Cook, uncovered, stirring occasionally, until tender. Drain in a colander. Divide the cooked noodles between 2 plates, top each piece of fish, and pour the pan juices over all. Saute the almonds in the same skillet with the butter. Sprinkle over the fish and serve.

Makes 2 servings. Each serving has 370 calories.

Note: The recipe may be halved to serve 1 or doubled to serve 4. Serve with cooked carrots and steamed asparagus.

HALIBUT NIÇOISE
ON GREEN NOODLES

   1 slice halibut, about ½ pounds
   1 small onion, sliced
   1 garlic clove, minced
   2 tomatoes, peeled and chopped
   ¼ cup dry white wine
   2 black olives, sliced
   1 anchovy fillet, drained and chopped
     Pinch of freshy ground black pepper
   4 ounces spinach fettucini
1 ½ quarts boiling water

Cut the halibut into large chunks. Put the fish in a nonstick frying pan. Add the onion slices, garlic, tomatoes, and white wine. Cover and poach over low heat for 5 to 7 minutes, or until the fish flakes easily. Add the sliced olives and anchovy and keep warm. Meanwhile, gradually add the fettucini to rapidly boiling water so that the water continues to boil. Cook, uncovered, stirring occasionally, until tender. Drain in a colander. Serve the fish and sauce over the cooked fettucini.

Makes 2 servings. Each serving has 415 calories.

Note: The recipe may be halved to serve 1 or doubled to serve 4. Serve with cooked spinach or turnip greens.

BUTTERMILK DILLED FLOUNDER ON LINGUINI

        1   slice flounder, about ½ pound
      ½   teaspoon dried dill
      ⅛   teaspoon paprika
        1   small onion, sliced
      ½   cup buttermilk
        4   ounces linguini
    1 ½   quarts boiling water

Cut the flounder in half and put it in a nonstick frying pan. Sprinkle with the dill and paprika. Put the onion slices around the fish. Pour the buttermilk around the fish. Cover and cook over low heat for 5 to 7 minutes, or until the fish flakes easily. Meanwhile, gradually add the linguini to rapidly boiling water so that the water continues to boil. Cook, uncovered, stirring occasionally, until tender. Drain in a colander. Serve the fish and sauce over the linguini.

Makes 2 servings. Each serving has 408 calories.

Note: The recipe may be halved to serve 1 or doubled to serve 4. Serve with cooked broccoli.

LINGUINI WITH FISH PROVENÇALE

 1 small onion, finely diced
 1 garlic clove, finely diced
 4 large mushrooms, sliced
 ½ cup chopped tomatoes
 ¼ cup dry white wine or water
 1 tablespoon chopped fresh parsley leaves
 ¼ teaspoon dried thyme
 ⅛ teaspoon freshly ground black pepper
 2 flounder fillets (about ¼ pound each)
 4 ounces linguini
1 ½ quarts boiling water

Put the onion, garlic, and mushrooms in a large frying pan. Add the tomatoes, wine, parsley, and thyme. Cover and cook for 4 minutes. Lay the fish on top of the sauce, cover, and cook for 8 to 10 minutes, or until the fish flakes easily. Meanwhile, gradually add the linguini to rapidly boiling water so that the water continues to boil. Cook, uncovered, stirring occasionally, until tender. Drain in a colander. Place half the linguini on each of two plates. Top with a piece of fish and the sauce.

Makes 2 servings. Each serving has 348 calories.

Note: The recipe may be halved to serve 1 or doubled to serve 4. Serve with cooked broccoli.

POACHED FISH ROLLS ON NOODLES

        2 flounder fillets (about ¼ pound each)
      ¼ cup dry white wine or water
      ½ cup peeled and chopped fresh tomatoes
        1 tablespoon fresh lemon juice
        1 tablespoon chopped onion
        1 tablespoon chopped fresh parsley leaves
        1 teaspoon dried dill
        4 ounces medium egg noodles
    1 ½ quarts boiling water
          Dash of freshly ground black pepper

Roll each fillet and place it in a frying pan. Add the wine, tomatoes, lemon juice, onion, parsley, and dill. Cover and simmer over low heat for 8 to 10 minutes, or until the fish flakes easily. Meanwhile, gradually add the medium egg noodles to rapidly boiling water so that the water continues to boil. Cook, uncovered, stirring occasionally, until tender. Drain in a colander and put half of the noodles on each plate. Top with a cooked fillet and some sauce.

Makes 2 servings. Each serving has 435 calories.

Note: The recipe may be halved to serve 1 or doubled to serve 4. Serve with cooked zucchini on the side.

SHRIMP PORTUGAISE ON BROAD NOODLES

      1 onion, finely diced
      1 green bell pepper, seeded and finely diced
      1 pimiento, diced
      1 8-ounce can tomato sauce
   ¼ cup fresh orange juice
   ½ teaspoon grated orange rind
   ½ pound shrimp, peeled and deveined
      4 ounces broad egg noodles
1 ½ quarts boiling water

Put the onion, green pepper, pimiento, tomato sauce, orange juice, and grated orange rind in a frying pan. Simmer for several minutes, or until the vegetables are limp. Add the shrimp and cook for 4 minutes, or until the shrimp turn pink. Meanwhile, gradually add the broad egg noodles to rapidly boiling water so that the water continues to boil. Cook, uncovered, stirring occasionally, until tender. Drain in a colander. Serve the shrimp sauce over noodles.

Makes 2 servings. Each serving has 413 calories.

Note: The recipe may be halved to serve 1 or doubled to serve 4.

BOUILLABAISSE ON LINGUINI

    6 fresh clams in the shell
    ¼ pound shrimp, peeled and deveined
    ⅓ pound halibut fillet, cut into chunks
    1 16-ounce can stewed whole tomatoes
      Dash of Tabasco sauce
    1 small onion, diced
    1 garlic clove, minced
    ¼ teaspoon dried thyme
    4 ounces linguini
 1 ½ quarts boiling water

Scrub the clam shells until all sand has been removed. Put the
clams, shrimp, and halibut into a saucepan. Add the tomatoes,
Tabasco sauce, onion, garlic, and thyme. Cover and simmer over
low heat about 5 to 7 minutes, until the shells open and the shrimp
turn pink. Meanwhile, gradually add the linguini to rapidly boiling
water so that the water continues to boil. Cook, uncovered, stirring
occasionally, until tender. Drain in a colander. Serve the Bouilla-
baisse on the linguini.

Makes 2 servings. Each serving has 497 calories.

Note: The recipe may be halved to serve 1 or doubled to serve 4.
Serve with a mixed fresh green salad with a low-calorie dressing.

SHRIMP IN CREAMY TOMATO SAUCE ON SPAGHETTI

- ½ pound shrimp, peeled and deveined
- 1 onion, thinly sliced
- 2 tablespoons Fat-Free White Sauce Mix (see recipe page 34)
- 1 16-ounce can whole tomatoes
- 1 tablespoon chopped fresh parsley leaves
- ⅛ teaspoon freshly ground black pepper
- 4 ounces spaghetti
- 1 ½ quarts boiling water

Boil the shrimp until they are pink, about 3 minutes. Drain. Put the onion in a nonstick frying pan and sauté until it is limp. Combine the white sauce mix with the tomatoes, parsley, and pepper. Pour over the onion and cook and stir until mixture thickens. Meanwhile, gradually add the spaghetti to rapidly boiling water so that the water continues to boil. Cook, uncovered, stirring occasionally, until tender. Drain in a colander. Add the shrimp to the tomato sauce and serve over the spaghetti.

Makes 2 servings. Each serving has 433 calories.

Note: The recipe may be halved to serve 1 or doubled to serve 4. Serve with a crisp green salad with a low-calorie dressing.

LINGUINI WITH SHRIMP SAUCE

   1 onion, diced
 ¼ pound fresh mushrooms, sliced
   1 green bell pepper, diced
   1 8-ounce can tomato sauce
 ¼ teaspoon Worcestershire sauce
 ½ pound cleaned, deveined cooked shrimp
   4 ounces linguini
1 ½ quarts boiling water
   2 tablespoons grated Parmesan cheese

Sauté the onion, mushrooms, and green pepper in a nonstick frying pan until they are limp. Stir frequently. Add the tomato sauce
and Worcestershire sauce, cover, and simmer for 5 minutes. Add
the cooked shrimp and heat through. Meanwhile, gradually add
the linguini to rapidly boiling water so that the water continues to
boil. Cook, uncovered, stirring occasionally, until tender. Drain in a
colander. Serve the cooked linguini topped with shrimp sauce.
Sprinkle with grated cheese.

Makes 2 servings. Each serving has 370 calories.

Note: The recipe may be halved to serve 1 or doubled to serve 4.
Serve with a fresh green salad topped with grated fresh carrots and
a low-calorie dressing.

PASTA SCAMPI

  1 **tablespoon olive oil**
  1 **garlic clove, minced**
 ½ **pound shrimp, peeled and cleaned**
 ¼ **cup dry white wine**
  1 **tablespoon fresh lemon juice**
 ¼ **teaspoon dried oregano**
  1 **tablespoon chopped fresh parsley leaves**
  4 **ounces spaghetti**
1 ½ **quarts boiling water**

Heat the oil in a nonstick frying pan. Add the garlic and shrimp and sauté stirring frequently, until the shrimp turn pink. Add the wine, lemon juice, oregano, and parsley and cook for several minutes longer. Meanwhile, gradually add the spaghetti to rapidly boiling water so that the water continues to boil. Cook, uncovered, stirring occasionally, until tender. Drain in a colander. Serve the spaghetti topped with the shrimp and any remaining liquid.

Makes 2 servings. Each serving has 385 calories.

Note: The recipe may be halved to serve 1 or doubled to serve 4.

LINGUINI WITH SHRIMP IN GREEN SAUCE

¼ cup dry white wine
1 tablespoon finely chopped fresh parsley leaves
1 tablespoon finely chopped watercress (optional)
1 small garlic clove, minced
1 small onion, finely diced
½ pound shrimp, peeled and deveined
1 tablespoon fresh lemon juice
Dash of Tabasco sauce
4 ounces linguini
1 ½ quarts boiling water

Put the wine, parsley, watercress, garlic, and onion in a nonstick frying pan. Simmer for several minutes. Add the shrimp, lemon juice, and Tabasco sauce. Cover and cook for 4 minutes, or until the shrimp are pink. Meanwhile, gradually add the linguini to rapidly boiling water so that the water continues to boil. Cook, uncovered, stirring occasionally, until tender. Drain in a colander. Serve the shrimp sauce over the cooked linguini.

Makes 2 servings. Each serving has 350 calories.

Note: The recipe may be halved to serve 1 or doubled to serve 4.

LINGUINI WITH SCALLOPS

    4 ounces linguini
1 ½ quarts boiling water
  ½ pound bay scallops
  ¼ cup dry white wine
    1 lemon wedge
  ¼ cup Fat-Free White Sauce Mix (see recipe page 34)
  ¼ cup clam juice
  ⅛ teaspoon dried thyme
       Dash of freshly ground black pepper

Gradually add the linguini to rapidly boiling water so that the water continues to boil. Cook, uncovered, stirring occasionally, until tender. Drain in a colander. Meanwhile, put the scallops and white wine in a frying pan. Squeeze the lemon over all. Cover and simmer for 3 to 4 minutes, or until the scallops are opaque. Combine white sauce mix with the clam juice, thyme, and pepper and mix until smooth. Then stir into the skillet. Cook for a moment to thicken. Toss with the linguini and serve.

Makes 2 servings. Each serving has 387 calories.

Note: The recipe may be halved to serve 1 or doubled to serve 4. Serve with cooked zucchini.

LINGUINI WITH SHRIMP MARINARA

4 ounces linguini
1 ½ quarts boiling water
1 cup Marinara Sauce (see recipe page 33), or
   commercial sauce
½ pound shrimp, peeled and deveined
1 tablespoon chopped fresh parsley leaves

Gradually add the linguini to rapidly boiling water so that the water
continues to boil. Cook, uncovered, stirring occasionally, until
tender. Drain in a colander. Meanwhile, pour the Marinara Sauce
into a frying pan. Bring the sauce to a boil and add the shrimp.
Cover and cook for 4 minutes, or until the shrimp are cooked
through and pink. Serve the sauce and shrimp on top of the linguini. Sprinkle chopped parsley on each serving.

Makes 2 servings. Each serving has 387 calories.

Note: The recipe may be halved to serve 1 or doubled to serve 4.
Serve with cooked carrots and peas.

SCALLOPS CACCIATORE WITH PASTA SHELLS

²/₃ pound sea or bay scallops
1 onion, diced
1 green bell pepper, diced
1 garlic clove, minced
1 16-ounce can whole tomatoes
1 bay leaf
1 tablespoon chopped fresh parsley leaves
⅛ teaspoon freshly ground black pepper
4 ounces pasta shells
1½ quarts boiling water

Rinse the scallops in cold water and remove any clinging bits of shell. Put the scallops in a nonstick frying pan. Add the remaining ingredients. Cook over low heat for 5 minutes, or until the scallops are cooked through. Meanwhile, gradually add the pasta shells to rapidly boiling water so that the water continues to boil. Cook, uncovered, stirring occasionally, until tender. Drain in a colander. Add the pasta shells to the frying pan, mix in thoroughly, and serve at once.

Makes 2 servings. Each serving has 423 calories.

Note: The recipe may be halved to serve 1 or doubled to serve 4. Serve with cooked string beans on the side.

CAVATELLI WITH
SHRIMP-YOGURT SAUCE

   4 ounces cavatelli
1 ½ quarts boiling water
  ½ cup plain low-fat yogurt
   6 large cooked shrimp
   1 tablespoon sliced scallion
   2 tablespoons chopped fresh parsley leaves
  ¼ teaspoon Worcestershire sauce

Gradually add the cavatelli to rapidly boiling water so that the water
continues to boil. Cook, uncovered, stirring occasionally, until
tender. Drain in a colander. Combine the yogurt, shrimp, scallion,
parsley, and Worcestershire sauce in a blender. Cover and blend
until almost smooth. Serve over the hot cavatelli.

Makes 2 servings. Each serving has 270 calories.

Note: The recipe may be halved to serve 1 or doubled to serve 4.
Serve with a mixed green salad with a low-calorie dressing.

SHRIMP RATATOUILLE ON NOODLES

- 1 small zucchini, sliced
- 1 cup peeled, diced eggplant
- 1 medium-sized onion, sliced
- 1 garlic clove, minced
- 2 tomatoes, cut in wedges
- 1 green bell pepper, diced
- 2 tablespoons tomato paste
- 1 tablespoon dry sherry (optional)
- ¼ teaspoon dried basil
- ⅓ pound raw shrimp, peeled and deveined
- 4 ounces broad egg noodles
- 1½ quarts boiling water

Put the zucchini, eggplant, onion, garlic, tomatoes, and green pepper in a large nonstick frying pan. Sauté the vegetables, stirring frequently, until they are limp. Add the tomato paste, sherry, and basil. Cover and simmer for 10 minutes. Add the shrimp, cover, and simmer for 4 minutes, or until the shrimp turn pink. Meanwhile, gradually add the broad egg noodles to rapidly boiling water so that the water continues to boil. Cook, uncovered, stirring occasionally, until tender. Drain in a colander. Serve the noodles topped with the shrimp sauce.

Makes 2 servings. Each serving has 393 calories.

Note: The recipe may be halved to serve 1 or doubled to serve 4. Serve with a crisp green salad with a low-calorie dressing.

FETTUCINI WITH CRABMEAT AND ASPARAGUS

    6 asparagus stalks, cut into 1-inch slices
    2 scallions, sliced
    3 ounces crabmeat
    1 tablespoon chopped fresh parsley leaves
  ¼ teaspoon dried basil
  ⅛ teaspoon freshly ground black pepper
    2 tablespoons Fat-Free White Sauce Mix (see recipe page 34)
  ½ cup water
    4 ounces fettucini
1 ½ quarts boiling water

Put the asparagus into a large frying pan. Add ½ inch of water and cook until the asparagus is just tender. Drain. Add the scallions, crabmeat, parsley, basil, and pepper. Combine the white sauce mix with the ½ cup water and add to the pan. Cook, stirring constantly, until the mixture has thickened. Meanwhile, gradually add the fettucini to rapidly boiling water so that the water continues to boil. Cook, uncovered, stirring occasionally, until tender. Drain in a colander. Serve the fettucini tossed with the crabmeat–asparagus sauce.

Makes 2 servings. Each serving has 290 calories.

Note: The recipe may be halved to serve 1 or doubled to serve 4.

CRAB MAISON ON BROAD NOODLES

¼ cup dry vermouth or dry white wine
1 tablespoon chopped fresh parsley leaves
½ teaspoon dried tarragon
1 scallion, finely sliced
3 ounces crabmeat
1 tablespoon fresh lemon juice
   Dash of Tabasco sauce
2 tablespoons Fat-Free White Sauce Mix (see recipe page 34)
½ cup water
4 ounces broad egg noodles
1 ½ quarts boiling water

Put the vermouth, parsley, tarragon, and scallion in a nonstick frying pan. Cook for several minutes. Add the crabmeat, lemon juice, and Tabasco sauce and cook for several minutes longer, or until the crabmeat is pink and hot. Combine the white sauce mix with the ½ cup water until smooth. Add to the frying pan and cook until the mixture has thickened. Meanwhile, gradually add the broad egg noodles to rapidly boiling water so that the water continues to boil. Cook, uncovered, stirring occasionally, until tender. Drain in a colander. Serve the crab mixture over the cooked noodles.

Makes 2 servings. Each serving has 283 calories.

Note: The recipe may be halved to serve 1 or doubled to serve 4.

CRABMEAT MACARONI SALAD

  ½ pound cooked or canned crabmeat
  4 ounces elbow macaroni
1 ½ quarts boiling water
  ½ cup plain low-fat yogurt
  ¼ teaspoon dried tarragon
  1 tablespoon chopped fresh or freeze-dried chives
  2 lettuce cups
  1 tablespoon chopped pimientos (optional)

Cut crabmeat into chunks, discarding any cartilage. Gradually add the elbow macaroni to rapidly boiling water so that the water continues to boil. Cook, uncovered, stirring occasionally, until tender. Drain in a colander. Add the crabmeat. Combine the yogurt, tarragon, and chives and mix through the crabmeat and macaroni. Spoon into lettuce cups and top each serving with chopped pimientos.

Makes 2 servings. Each serving has 390 calories.

Note: The recipe may be halved to serve 1 or doubled to serve 4. Garnish with carrot and celery sticks.

BAKED OYSTERS AND NOODLES

     4 ounces medium egg noodles
1 ½ quarts boiling water
     ¼ cup Fat-Free White Sauce Mix (see recipe page 34)
     1 cup tomato juice
     1 teaspoon chopped fresh parsley leaves
     ⅛ teaspoon freshly ground black pepper
     1 cup (about ½ pound) fresh shucked oysters
     ¼ cup Italian-style seasoned bread crumbs

Gradually add the medium egg noodles to rapidly boiling water so that the water continues to boil. Cook, uncovered, stirring occasionally, until tender. Drain in a colander. Combine the white sauce mix with the tomato juice, parsley, and pepper. Add to the noodles along with the oysters. Pour all into a greased 1-quart casserole and top with the bread crumbs. Bake in a 425-degree oven for 20 minutes, or until the topping is lightly browned.

Makes 2 servings. Each serving has 380 calories.

Note: The recipe may be halved to serve 1 or doubled to serve 4. Serve with cooked spinach on the side.

STEWED OYSTERS ON LINGUINI

    1 **cup fresh shucked oysters**
    ¼ **cup cold water**
    1 **cup scalded skim milk**
    ⅛ **teaspoon freshly ground black pepper**
    4 **ounces linguini**
1 ½ **quarts boiling water**

Put the oysters into a strainer over a large saucepan. Pour the ¼ cup cold water over oysters, allowing the liquid to drain into the saucepan. Remove any clinging bits of shell and add the oysters to the saucepan. Add the scalded milk and the pepper. Simmer for 3 to 5 minutes, or until edges of the oysters begin to curl. Meanwhile, gradually add the linguini to rapidly boiling water so that the water continues to boil. Cook, uncovered, stirring occasionally, until tender. Drain in a colander. Serve the linguini topped with the oysters and the pan liquid.

Makes 2 servings. Each serving has 335 calories.

Note: The recipe may be halved to serve 1 or doubled to serve 4. Serve with cooked spinach on the side.

ZUPPA DI CLAMS ON LINGUINI

  1 **dozen fresh clams**
  1 **cup tomato juice**
  ½ **cup bottled clam juice**
  ¼ **teaspoon dried oregano**
  ⅛ **teaspoon dried thyme**
  ⅛ **teaspoon garlic powder**
  4 **ounces linguini**
1 ½ **quarts boiling water**

Wash the clams just before cooking. Combine the tomato juice, clam juice, oregano, thyme, and garlic powder in a large frying pan. Stir well. Add the clams in the shell. Cover and cook for 5 to 8 minutes, or until all the shells have opened. Discard any unopened clams. Meanwhile, gradually add the linguini to rapidly boiling water so that the water continues to boil. Cook, uncovered, stirring occasionally, until tender. Drain in a colander. Serve the clams and sauce over the cooked linguini.

Makes 2 servings. Each serving has 335 calories.

Note: The recipe may be halved to serve 1 or doubled to serve 4. Serve in a soup bowl so the liquid may be eaten with a spoon. Follow with a crisp green salad with a low-calorie dressing.

LINGUINI AND MUSSELS MARINARA

4 ounces linguini
1 ½ quarts boiling water
1 cup Marinara Sauce (see recipe page 33) or
commercial sauce
1 pound mussels in shells

Gradually add the linguini to rapidly boiling water so that the water continues to boil. Cook, uncovered, stirring occasionally, until tender. Drain in a colander. Meanwhile, pour the Marinara Sauce into a frying pan. Scrub the mussel shells very well and put them in the sauce. Heat, covered, until the shells open. Serve the mussels in the shells and the sauce on top of the linguini.

Makes 2 servings. Each serving has 357 calories.

Note: The recipe may be halved to serve 1 or doubled to serve 4. Serve with cooked spinach or turnip greens.

SPAGHETTI WITH FLORENTINE CLAM SAUCE

1 10-ounce package frozen chopped spinach, thawed
1 onion, diced
1 garlic clove, minced
¼ cup dry white wine
1 5-ounce can minced clams with juice
¼ teaspoon dried thyme
4 ounces thin spaghetti
1½ quarts boiling water
2 tablespoons grated Romano cheese

Drain the spinach and put it in a nonstick frying pan. Add the onion and garlic and cook for several minutes, stirring constantly. Add the wine, clams with their juice, and the thyme. Cover and cook for 3 minutes. Meanwhile, gradually add the thin spaghetti to rapidly boiling water so that the water continues to boil. Cook, uncovered, stirring occasionally, until tender. Drain in a colander. Toss the spaghetti with spinach sauce and serve, sprinkled with the grated cheese.

Makes 2 servings. Each serving has 344 calories.

Note: The recipe may be halved to serve 1 or doubled to serve 4. Serve with a fresh green salad, topped with finely sliced celery and a low-calorie dressing.

TUNA–ZITI MARINARA

  1 **7-ounce can water-packed tuna**
  1 **cup Marinara Sauce (see recipe page 33) or**
       commercial product
  ¼ **teaspoon garlic powder**
  ¼ **teaspoon dried basil**
  4 **ounces ziti**
1½ **quarts boiling water**
  2 **tablespoons grated Parmesan cheese**

Drain the tuna and cut it into chunks. Heat the Marinara Sauce, garlic powder, and basil in a saucepan. Add the tuna. Meanwhile, gradually add the ziti to rapidly boiling water so that the water continues to boil. Cook, uncovered, stirring occasionally, until tender. Drain in a colander. Toss with the tuna–marinara sauce and serve sprinkled with grated Parmesan cheese.

Make 2 servings. Each serving has 418 calories.

Note: The recipe may be halved to serve 1 or doubled to serve 4.

SAUCY TUNA ON GREEN NOODLES

    1   7-ounce can water-packed tuna
    1   onion, thinly sliced
    1   8-ounce can tomato sauce
    ¼   teaspoon dried oregano
    ¼   teaspoon dried basil
        Dash of freshly ground black pepper
    4   ounces spinach fettucini
 1 ½   quarts boiling water

Drain the tuna and cut it into chunks. Simmer the onion, tomato sauce, oregano, basil, and pepper in a saucepan for about 5 minutes, stirring occasionally. Add the tuna. Meanwhile, gradually add the fettucini to rapidly boiling water so that the water continues to boil. Cook, uncovered, stirring occasionally, until tender. Drain in a colander. Serve the fettucini topped with the tuna sauce.

Make 2 servings. Each serving has 395 calories.

Note: The recipe may be halved to serve 1 or doubled to serve 4.

PASTA AND TUNA POSITANO

    4 ounces large pasta shells
1 ½ quarts boiling water
    1 3-ounce can water-packed tuna, drained
    ½ cup frozen peas, thawed
    1 tomato, peeled and chopped
    2 pitted black olives, sliced
    ½ cup part skim ricotta
    1 tablespoon grated Parmesan cheese
    ¼ teaspoon dried basil
    ¼ teaspoon garlic powder
    ½ pound fresh asparagus, cooked and cooled

Gradually add the pasta shells to rapidly boiling water so that the water continues to boil. Cook, uncovered, stirring occasionally, until tender. Drain in a colander and cool. Break the tuna into chunks and add it to the cooled pasta shells with the thawed peas, tomato, and olives. Combine ricotta, Parmesan cheese, basil, and garlic powder in an electric blender. Pour over the pasta mixture. Arrange the salad on the cooked asparagus spears.

Make 2 servings. Each serving has 400 calories.

Note: The recipe may be halved to serve 1 or doubled to serve 4. Serve with a salad of crisp greens if desired.

TUNA–NOODLE CASSEROLE

    4 ounces broad egg noodles
1 ½ quarts boiling water
    1 7-ounce can water-packed tuna, drained and flaked
   ½ teaspoon celery salt
   ⅛ teaspoon freshly ground black pepper
   ⅛ teaspoon dried thyme
    1 cup tomato juice

Gradually add the broad egg noodles to rapidly boiling water so that the water continues to boil. Cook, uncovered, stirring occasionally, until tender. Drain in a colander. Pour half the noodles into the bottom of a small greased 1-quart casserole. Top with the flaked tuna, celery salt, pepper, and thyme. Cover with the remaining noodles. Pour the tomato juice over the top. Bake in a 350-degree oven for 20 minutes, or until the top noodles are lightly browned.

Make 2 servings. Each serving has 360 calories.

Note: Extra portions may be refrigerated for up to 3 days or frozen up to 2 months. Serve with a fresh fruit salad.

TUNA–PASTA SALAD

      4 ounces pasta spirals
1 ½ quarts boiling water
      1 3-ounce can water-packed tuna, drained and flaked
   ½ zucchini, diced
   ½ green bell pepper, diced
      2 scallions, sliced
      1 tablespoon capers, rinsed and drained
      1 tablespoon vegetable oil
      1 tablespoon fresh lemon juice
   ⅛ teaspoon dried basil
   ⅛ teaspoon dried oregano
   ⅛ teaspoon freshly ground black pepper

Gradually add the pasta spirals to rapidly boiling water so that the water continues to boil. Cook, uncovered, stirring occasionally, until tender. Drain in a colander and chill. In a large bowl, toss together the pasta, flaked tuna, zucchini, green pepper, scallions, and capers. Combine the oil, lemon juice, basil, oregano, and pepper. Pour the dressing over the pasta mixture and toss lightly. Chill until ready to serve.

Makes 2 servings. Each serving has 343 calories.

Note: The recipe may be halved to serve 1 or doubled to serve 4. Serve on a bed of lettuce cups with wedges of ripe tomatoes as garnish.

TUNA–FETTUCINI SALAD

> 4 ounces narrow egg noodles
> 1 ½ quarts boiling water
> 1 7-ounce can tuna in oil
> 1 small garlic clove, minced
> 2 ounces fresh mushrooms, sliced
> 1 cup fresh broccoli flowerets
> ½ zucchini, sliced
> 1 small red bell pepper, diced
> 1 tablespoon chopped fresh parsley leaves
> ¼ teaspoon dried basil
> ⅛ teaspoon freshly ground black pepper
> 1 teaspoon fresh lemon juice
> 1 slice (1 ounce) Swiss cheese, shredded

Gradually add the narrow egg noodles to rapidly boiling water so that the water continues to boil. Cook, uncovered, stirring occasionally, until tender. Drain in a colander and cool. Meanwhile, drain the oil from the tuna into a large frying pan. Put the tuna in a bowl and break into chunks. Set aside. Add the garlic, mushrooms, broccoli, zucchini, red pepper, parsley, and basil to the tuna oil in the frying pan. Sauté over low heat, stirring until vegetables are tender, about 4 to 5 minutes. Add this mixture to tuna chunks. Add cooked noodles, pepper, and lemon juice and toss well. Cover and chill. Just before serving, top with the shredded cheese.

Makes 2 servings. Each serving has 430 calories.

Note: The recipe may be halved to serve 1 or doubled to serve 4. Arrange the salad on a bed of escarole or lettuce leaves and garnish with cherry tomatoes, if desired.

CHEESE AND TUNA PASTA PUDDING

    2 ounces vermicelli noodles or very thin spaghetti
    1 quart boiling water
    ½ cup skim milk
    1 egg
    1 3-ounce can water-packed tuna, drained and flaked
    ½ cup part skim ricotta
    ¼ cup fresh mushrooms, sliced
    2 fresh scallions, sliced
    1 small garlic clove, finely minced
    ¼ teaspoon dried tarragon
    1 tablespoon grated Parmesan cheese

Gradually add the vermicelli to rapidly boiling water so that the water continues to boil. Cook, uncovered, stirring occasionally, until tender. Drain in a colander. In a large bowl, beat the milk and egg together. Stir in the flaked tuna, cooked noodles, ricotta, mushrooms, scallions, garlic, and tarragon. Mix well. Pour into a lightly greased, small, shallow baking dish. Sprinkle with Parmesan cheese. Place in a larger pan filled with 1 inch of hot water. Bake in a 350-degree oven for 35 minutes, or until a knife inserted in the center comes out clean. Let stand for 10 minutes before serving.

Makes 2 servings. Each serving has 300 calories.

Note: The recipe may be doubled to serve 4. Extra portions of this recipe may be refrigerated for up to 3 days and reheated.

PASTA RIVIERA

    4 ounces small pasta shells
1 ½ quarts boiling water
    ¼ cup dry white wine
    1 garlic clove, finely minced
    1 green bell pepper, seeded and cut into strips
    1 red bell pepper, seeded and cut into strips
    1 small zucchini, sliced
    1 7-ounce can water-packed tuna, drained and
        broken into chunks
    2 tablespoons chopped fresh parsley leaves
    1 tablespoon drained capers
    ½ teaspoon dried thyme
    ½ cup cherry tomatoes, halved

Gradually add the small pasta shells to rapidly boiling water so that the water continues to boil. Cook, uncovered, stirring occasionally, until tender. Drain in a colander. Meanwhile, pour the wine into a large frying pan. Add the garlic, green and red peppers, and zucchini. Cook and stir until the vegetables are just tender. Stir in tuna, parsley, capers, and thyme. Cook until just heated through. Add the cooked pasta shells to the pan and mix thoroughly. Just before serving, add the halved cherry tomatoes.

Makes 2 servings. Each serving has 375 calories.

Note: The recipe may be halved to serve 1 or doubled to serve 4. Serve with a crisp mixed green salad with a low-calorie dressing.

BROAD EGG NOODLES
WITH SALMON SAUCE

   ¼ **cup Fat-Free White Sauce Mix (see recipe page 34)**
   1 **7-ounce can salmon**
   1 **tablespoon butter or margarine**
   1 **tablespoon dry sherry (optional)**
     Dash of freshly ground black pepper
   4 **ounces broad egg noodles**
1 ½ **quarts boiling water**

Put the white sauce mix into a saucepan. Drain the liquid from the
salmon into a measuring cup. Fill the cup with water to make 1 cup.
Stir the liquid into the sauce mix until smooth. Add the butter and
cook over low heat, stirring constantly, until the mixture has thickened. Add the sherry and pepper and cook for several minutes
longer. Add the flaked salmon to the sauce. Meanwhile, gradually
add the broad egg noodles to rapidly boiling water so that the water
continues to boil. Cook, uncovered, stirring occasionally, until
tender. Drain in a colander. Put the noodles on a platter and top
with salmon sauce.

Makes 2 servings. Each serving has 465 calories.

Note: The recipe may be halved to serve 1 or doubled to serve 4.
Garnish with parsley. Serve with romaine lettuce and cherry
tomatoes.

SALMON DIVAN ON NOODLES

   4 ounces broad egg noodles
1 ½ quarts boiling water
   1 10-ounce package frozen broccoli spears, thawed
   1 7 ¾-ounce can salmon, drained and broken into chunks
  ¼ cup Fat-Free White Sauce Mix (see recipe page 34)
   1 cup tomato juice
  ¼ teaspoon dried dill
     Pinch of freshly ground black pepper

Gradually add the broad egg noodles to rapidly boiling water so that the water continues to boil. Cook, uncovered, stirring occasionally, until tender. Drain in a colander and transfer to the bottom of a greased 1-quart casserole. Top with the thawed broccoli. Arrange the chunks of salmon over the broccoli. Combine the white sauce mix with the tomato juice, dill, and pepper. Pour the sauce over all. Bake in a 350-degree oven for 25 minutes, or until hot and bubbly.

Makes 2 servings. Each serving has 446 calories.

Note: The recipe may be halved to serve 1 or doubled to serve 4. Serve with a crisp green salad with red onion slices and a low-calorie dressing.

SALMON AND SHELL SALAD

    4 ounces small pasta shells
1 ½ quarts boiling water
    1 7-ounce can salmon
    1 green bell pepper, diced
    1 carrot, grated
    3 radishes, thinly sliced
   ¼ cup plain low-fat yogurt
    1 teaspoon dried dill
   ¼ teaspoon dry mustard
       Dash of Worcestershire sauce

Gradually add the small pasta shells to rapidly boiling water so that the water continues to boil. Cook, uncovered, stirring occasionally, until tender. Drain in a colander. Remove any skin and bones from the salmon and break it into chunks. Add the pasta shells, green pepper, carrot, and radishes. Combine the yogurt, dill, mustard, and Worcestershire sauce. Mix gently through the salmon mixture.

Makes 2 servings. Each serving has 360 calories.

Note: The recipe may be halved to serve 1 or doubled to serve 4. Serve on a bed of lettuce surrounded with tomato wedges.

Ten

Low-Calorie Vegetable Side Dishes

If you are really interested in balanced nutrition, you should know that it can only happen when you eat naturally colorful food. Most of nature's lovely colors are found in vegetables, as are a variety of important nutrients. So think of a colorful platter when you plan your menu for lunch and dinner.

Most vegetables are low in calories—about 20 or so calories per half cup. It's the added butter that makes vegetables seem to push calorie totals upward. Skip the butter and add herbs instead.

Vegetables should be steamed or cooked in a small amount of water only until crunchy. When you overcook vegetables, they lose valuable vitamins and minerals and become soggy and tasteless. If possible, try to use only fresh vegetables. If you can't, then choose frozen plain vegetables (unsauced and unsalted), or if you must, canned vegetables in the new salt-free varieties whenever possible.

Keep some raw celery and carrot sticks in the refrigerator for moments when you must munch something. Rotate the kinds of vegetables you buy, so you are sure to get a good mix of nutrients within every few days. Try to eat a dark green or yellow vegetable at least every other day for Vitamin A.

For mixed green salads, buy fresh lettuce every few days. Wash it and pat it dry with paper toweling and then store it in a plastic bag with a fresh piece of paper toweling to keep it crisp, or wrap it in a linen towel before refrigerating.

Sliced cucumbers, radishes, red onion, and grated carrot will all help to keep your salads varied and different. Coleslaw is also low in calories if you make it with plain low-fat yogurt rather than high-fat mayonnaise.

The higher-calorie vegetables are corn, lima beans and dried beans, peas, parsnips, avocado, white potatoes, and sweet potatoes. Low-calorie vegetables that are suitable for this diet are asparagus, green beans, beets, broccoli, Brussels sprouts, cabbage, carrots, cauliflower, celery, cucumbers, eggplant, lettuce, mushrooms, onions, sweet green and red peppers, radishes, spinach, squash, tomatoes, and turnips. Whenever possible, try to eat some of these vegetables uncooked.

This chapter is filled with tantalizing new ways to prepare low-calorie vegetables whenever you have the whim for adding some extra zest to your cooking.

LEMON ASPARAGUS

½ **pound fresh asparagus**
2 **cups water**
1 **teaspoon butter**
2 **tablespoons fresh lemon juice**

Trim the asparagus, removing the scales and hardened ends. Wash and tie together. Stand the asparagus in the bottom of a double boiler. Add water to a depth of 2 inches. Cover with the top of the double boiler turned upside down to provide a tall narrow cooking vessel. (This method boils the coarser asparagus bottoms while steaming the tender tips.) Cook for 15 minutes, or until tender, depending on the thickness of the stalks. Drain and place on a platter. Dot with the butter and sprinkle with the lemon juice.

Makes 2 servings. Each serving has 50 calories.

GREEN BEANS AMANDINE

1 **10-ounce package frozen whole green beans**
¼ **teaspoon dried marjoram**
⅛ **teaspoon freshly ground black pepper**
2 **tablespoons sliced blanched almonds**

Put the green beans in a saucepan with ½ inch of water. Add marjoram and pepper. Cover and cook for 5 minutes, or until tender. Drain. Serve with a sprinkling of sliced almonds.

Makes 2 servings. Each serving has 46 calories.

GREEN BEANS AND WATER CHESTNUTS

1 10-ounce package frozen cut green beans
2 canned water chestnuts, sliced thin
¼ teaspoon dried thyme
⅛ teaspoon freshly ground black pepper

Steam the green beans or cook in water until tender. Drain. Add the sliced chestnuts, thyme, and pepper and mix thoroughly.

Makes 2 servings. Each serving has 38 calories.

GREEN BEANS OREGANO

½ pound fresh green beans, or 1 10-ounce package frozen green beans
1 cup tomato juice
⅛ teaspoon freshly ground black pepper
¼ teaspoon dried oregano

Put the green beans in a saucepan and add the tomato juice, pepper, and oregano. Cover and simmer, stirring occasionally, for 10 minutes or until the beans are tender.

Makes 2 servings. Each serving has 60 calories.

BRUSSELS SPROUTS

1 10-ounce package frozen Brussels sprouts, or 1 cup fresh
  Brussels sprouts
½ cup water
½ teaspoon chopped fresh parsley leaves
1 teaspoon fresh lemon juice
⅛ teaspoon freshly ground black pepper

If the sprouts are fresh, trim and wash them well. Cut the sprouts in
half lengthwise and put them in a saucepan with the water, parsley,
lemon juice, and pepper. Cook for 5 minutes, or until the sprouts
are tender but not mushy. Drain.

Makes 2 servings. Each serving has 51 calories.

CARROTS AND MUSHROOMS TARRAGON

2 large carrots
½ cup water
½ teaspoon dried tarragon
1 teaspoon butter
¼ cup sliced fresh mushrooms

Pare the carrots and cut them into ¼-inch-thick slices. Put the
slices in a saucepan with the water and tarragon. Cover and cook
over medium heat for 15 minutes, or until they are tender. While
the carrots are cooking, melt the butter in a nonstick frying pan.
Add the mushrooms and cook until tender, stirring occasionally.
Drain the carrots and add them to the mushrooms.

Makes 2 servings. Each serving has 57 calories.

CARROT STRIPS

> 2 **large carrots, cut in lengthwise strips about 4 inches long**
> 1 **teaspoon chopped fresh parsley leaves**
> ¼ **cup water**
> 1 **teaspoon fresh lemon juice**
> 2 **teaspoons butter**

Put the carrots strips, parsley, and water in a saucepan. Cover and simmer for 15 minutes, or until the carrots are tender, adding a little more water if necessary. Drain. Add the lemon juice and butter. Heat and mix until the butter has melted.

Makes 2 servings. Each serving has 64 calories.

SHREDDED CARROTS AND RAISINS

> 2 **cups shredded carrots**
> ½ **cup water**
> 1 **tablespoon chopped fresh parsley leaves**
> 1 **tablespoon fresh lemon juice**
> 1 **tablespoon raisins**

Put the carrots, water, parsley, lemon juice, and raisins in a saucepan. Cover and cook over low heat for 15 minutes, or until the carrots are tender. Drain.

Makes 2 servings. Each serving has 46 calories.

Note: The recipe may be halved to serve 1 or doubled to serve 4.

CAULIFLOWER SALAD

- 1 **cup sliced raw cauliflower**
- 1 **tomato, cut in wedges**
- 2 **tablespoons Lemon French Dressing (see recipe page 169)**
- 1 **tablespoon chopped fresh or freeze-dried chives**
- ¼ **head lettuce, shredded**

Combine the cauliflower and tomatoes. Add the dressing and toss well. Chill for at least 1 hour. Just before serving, combine with the chives and lettuce.

Make 2 servings. Each serving has 61 calories.

WALDORF SALAD

- 1 **apple, pared and diced**
- 2 **tablespoons fresh lemon juice**
- ½ **cup thinly sliced celery**
- 2 **tablespoons broken walnuts**
- ¼ **cup plain low-fat yogurt**
- ¼ **teaspoon grated lemon rind**
- 2 **lettuce cups**

Combine the apple with the lemon juice and toss well to prevent browning. Add the celery and nuts. Add the yogurt and grated lemon rind and mix well. Spoon into the lettuce cups.

Makes 2 servings. Each serving has 67 calories.

COLESLAW

1 small head green cabbage, shredded
1 carrot, scraped and grated
1 green bell pepper, finely diced
¼ cup thinly sliced scallions
1 cup plain low-fat yogurt
¼ teaspoon dry mustard
1 tablespoon fresh lemon juice
1 teaspoon sugar

Combine the cabbage, carrot, green pepper, and scallions. In a separate bowl, combine the yogurt, mustard, lemon juice, and sugar. Mix the dressing with the cabbage mixture. Cover the refrigerate for several hours before serving.

Makes 6 servings. Each serving has 42 calories.

PICKLED CUCUMBER SALAD

1 cucumber, peeled and thinly sliced
1 onion, thinly sliced
¼ cup tarragon vinegar
¼ cup water
1 teaspoon dried dill
⅛ teaspoon freshly ground black pepper

Combine all the ingredients in a bowl. Cover and marinate in the refrigerator for several hours before serving. May be refrigerated for up to 5 days.

Makes 4 servings. Each serving has 17 calories.

CRISP CABBAGE SALAD

1 medium-sized head green cabbage, shredded
1 small onion, thinly sliced
1 green bell pepper, thinly sliced
2 carrots, grated
½ teaspoon celery seed
¼ cup wine vinegar
1 teaspoon sugar
1 cup water
⅛ teaspoon freshly ground black pepper

Combine the cabbage, onion, green pepper, and carrots. Mix well.
Combine the celery seed, vinegar, sugar, water, and black pepper.
Mix well and pour over cabbage mixture. Toss, cover, and chill for
several hours before serving.

Makes 6 servings. Each serving has 52 calories.

CUCUMBERS WITH YOGURT DRESSING

1 medium-sized cucumber, pared and thinly sliced
1 tablespoon cider vinegar
1 teaspoon chopped fresh or ¼ teaspoon dried dill
½ cup plain low-fat yogurt
1 small garlic clove, crushed

Put the sliced cucumbers in a small deep bowl. Combine the
vinegar, dill, yogurt, and garlic. Mix well. Toss the cucumbers with
yogurt mixture. Cover and chill.

Makes 2 servings. Each serving has 32 calories.

MUSHROOM SALAD

¼ small head iceberg lettuce
1 teaspoon chopped fresh or frozen chives
3 large mushrooms, sliced paper thin
2 teaspoons fresh lemon juice
2 tablespoons Lemon French Dressing
(see recipe page 000)

Tear up the lettuce into a salad bowl. Add the chives. Toss the sliced mushrooms with lemon juice and add them to the salad bowl. Add the dressing and toss.

Makes 2 servings. Each serving has 26 calories.

TENDER PEAS ROSEMARY

¾ pound fresh peas, shelled, or 1 10-ounce package frozen peas
1 cup water
¼ teaspoon dried rosemary
½ teaspoon sugar

Put the peas in a saucepan. Add the water, rosemary, and sugar. Bring to a boil, lower the heat, cover, and simmer for 10 minutes, or until the peas are tender. Drain.

Makes 2 servings. Each serving has 108 calories.

YOGURT CREAMED SPINACH

1 10-ounce package frozen chopped spinach
½ teaspoon onion powder
¼ teaspoon ground nutmeg
¼ cup plain low-fat yogurt

Put the spinach in a saucepan and add 1 inch of water. Add the onion powder and nutmeg. Cover and cook until tender. Drain. Stir in the yogurt.

Makes 2 servings. Each serving has 47 calories.

FRESH SPINACH SALAD

¼ pound fresh spinach, trimmed and washed
½ garlic clove, cut in half
4 slices red onion, separated into rings
2 large mushrooms, thinly sliced
¼ cup tomato juice
2 tablespoons wine vinegar
1 tablespoon olive oil
¼ teaspoon dry mustard
⅛ teaspoon dried tarragon

Tear the spinach leaves into bite-sized pieces. Rub a salad bowl with the cut garlic and discard the garlic. Fill the bowl with the torn spinach leaves. Add the red onion rings and sliced mushrooms. Combine the tomato juice, vinegar, oil, mustard, and tarragon. Shake well and pour over salad. Toss and serve.

Makes 2 servings. Each serving has 88 calories.

ITALIAN GREENS

  ½ pound fresh collard, kale, or turnip greens
  1 small garlic clove, crushed
1 ½ teaspoons olive oil
  ⅛ teaspoon freshly ground black pepper
  1 tablespoon grated Parmesan cheese
     Red onion rings

Trim and wash the greens well. Mix the garlic, oil, and pepper in a
shallow saucepan. Add trimmed greens and cover with ½ inch of
water. Bring to a boil, cover, lower the heat; cook until tender. Turn
into a serving dish and sprinkle with the cheese. Top with raw red
onion rings.

Makes 2 servings. Each serving has 85 calories.

ZESTY CHERRY TOMATOES

  1 cup cherry tomatoes
  2 tablespoons fresh lemon juice
  1 teaspoon olive oil
  ¼ teaspoon dried basil
  ¼ teaspoon dried thyme
  ⅛ teaspoon garlic powder
  1 tablespoon chopped fresh parsley leaves

Wash tomatoes and remove the stems. Put the tomatoes in a bowl.
Combine the remaining ingredients and pour over tomatoes. Toss
lightly. Cover and chill until ready to serve.

Makes 2 servings. Each serving has 35 calories.

BROILED TOMATOES

1 **medium-sized tomato**
2 **teaspoons Italian-style seasoned bread crumbs**
1 **teaspoon butter**

Cut the tomato in half and put it cut side up on a broiler pan. Top with the bread crumbs and a few dots of butter. Broil for 4 to 5 minutes, or until the tops are browned and bubbly, but the tomatoes are still firm.

Makes 2 servings. Each serving has 37 calories.

BAKED TOMATOES
WITH GREEN PEPPER TOPPING

2 **tomatoes**
½ **green bell pepper**
1 **tablespoon finely minced onion**
1 **teaspoon prepared mustard**
1 **tablespoon fine bread crumbs**

Cut the tomatoes in half and put them cut side up on a flat baking dish. Remove the seeds from pepper and chop the pepper very fine. Add the onion. Spread the mustard over the cut side of the tomatoes. Top each tomato half with the green pepper mixture. Sprinkle each with bread crumbs. Bake in a 375-degree oven for 15 minutes.

Makes 4 servings. Each serving has 25 calories.

ZUCCHINI

    1 **large zucchini, sliced thin**
    2 **celery stalks, sliced**
    1 **small onion, sliced**
    1 **8-ounce can tomato sauce**
  ¼ **teaspoon dried thyme**

Put all the ingredients into a saucepan and mix well. Cook over low heat for 15 minutes, or until the vegetables are tender.

Makes 2 servings. Each serving has 60 calories.

Note: The recipe may be doubled to serve 4.

ZUCCHINI MEDLEY

    1 **zucchini, thinly sliced**
    1 **small onion, thinly sliced**
    2 **celery stalks, thinly sliced**
  ¼ **cup sliced fresh mushrooms**
  ¼ **teaspoon dried thyme**
  ¼ **teaspoon paprika**
  ⅛ **teaspoon freshly ground black pepper**

Put all the ingredients into a large saucepan. Add ½ inch of water. Cover and simmer over low heat for 5 minutes, or until the vegetables are just tender.

Makes 2 servings. Each serving has 40 calories.

Eleven

Low-Calorie
Salad Dressings

If you stop using high-oil-content dressings on your salads you may be able to eliminate several hundred calories from your daily intake. There are low-calorie dressings available in your local super-market and you may want to try some of them. However, it's quite easy to make your own with low-fat ingredients, herbs, and spices. The advantage to making your own is that they will not have the gums, fillers, and preservatives found in the commercial products.

Most of the homemade dressings in this chapter will last for a week or more in the refrigerator. Don't let yourself get in a rut by eating the same kind of salad with the same kind of dressing every day. If variety is the spice of life in normal times, it's even more so when you embark upon a period of dieting and supposed deprivation. Of course, in the case of this particular diet, you shouldn't feel deprived at all. Instead, you should feel that you are going to have some fun with a diet for once.

If you are eating in a restaurant, refuse the prepared dressings and ask for cruets of vinegar and oil. (Use as much vinegar as you like, hoping that it's at least a good grade of wine vinegar, but use only 1 teaspoon of oil.) Or ask for some lemon wedges that can do wonders in perking up the natural goodness of garden greens.

You should have at least one raw vegetable salad each day to provide fiber and roughage in your diet. Sprinkle a tablespoon of wheat germ on the salad whenever you can. It will taste crunchy and will add extra bulk to your intake, besides adding Vitamin B's for your nutritional well-being.

Salads will be easier to make at the last minute if you have washed and crisped your lettuce as suggested in the chapter on vegetables. Here are some low-calorie dressing recipes in which the unnecessary oil has been eliminated and replaced with some very clever ingredients to please your palate.

OIL-FREE SALAD DRESSING

4 ounces red wine vinegar
4 ounces water
½ teaspoon sugar
¼ teaspoon salt
⅛ teaspoon dried oregano
⅛ teaspoon freshly ground black pepper
⅛ teaspoon garlic powder

Combine all the ingredients and mix vigorously before pouring over the salad.

Makes ½ cup dressing. Each tablespoon has 2 calories.

TOMATO JUICE SALAD DRESSING

1 cup salt-free tomato juice
3 tablespoons white wine vinegar
3 tablespoons salad oil
1 garlic clove, crushed
4 teaspoons sugar
2 teaspoons minced fresh parsley leaves
2 teaspoons dry white wine
2 teaspoons chopped scallion
¼ teaspoon freshly ground black pepper
¼ teaspoon dried tarragon
¼ teaspoon dry mustard

Put all ingredients into a screw-top jar and shake well. Use as a dressing for salad greens.

Makes about 1⅓ cups dressing.
Each tablespoon of dressing has 22 calories.

FRENCH DRESSING

³⁄₄ cup rice vinegar
2 tablespoons salad oil
2 tablespoons thawed apple juice concentrate
1 garlic clove, minced
¹⁄₄ teaspoon dry mustard
¹⁄₄ teaspoon paprika
¹⁄₈ teaspoon freshly ground black pepper

Combine all the ingredients in a screw-top jar. Shake well. Refrigerate until ready to use.

Makes 1 cup dressing. Each tablespoon has 17 calories.

VINAIGRETTE DRESSING

1 egg yolk
¹⁄₄ teaspoon garlic powder
¹⁄₂ teaspoon dry mustard
¹⁄₈ teaspoon freshly ground black pepper
2 tablespoons olive oil
1 tablespoon fresh lemon juice
¹⁄₄ cup red wine vinegar

Combine the egg yolk, garlic powder, mustard, and pepper in a blender. Drizzle in the olive oil until absorbed. Add the lemon juice and vinegar and blend well. Refrigerate until ready to use.

Makes about ¹⁄₂ cup of dressing. Each tablespoon has 35 calories.

LEMON FRENCH DRESSING

1 teaspoon unflavored gelatin
1 tablespoon cold water
¼ cup boiling water
1 tablespoon sugar
½ teaspoon salt
1 teaspoon grated lemon rind
½ cup fresh lemon juice
¼ teaspoon garlic powder
⅛ teaspoon freshly ground black pepper
⅛ teaspoon dry mustard
¼ teaspoon Worcestershire sauce

Soften the gelatin in the tablespoon of cold water. Add the boiling water and stir until the gelatin dissolves. Stir in sugar and salt until dissolved. Add the remaining ingredients and mix well. Chill until ready to serve. If mixture solidifies, put the container of dressing in a pan of hot water for 5 minutes.

Makes about 1 cup of dressing. Each tablespoon has 12 calories.

RUSSIAN–YOGURT DRESSING

½ cup plain low-fat yogurt
2 tablespoons chili sauce
1 teaspoon fresh lemon juice
⅛ teaspoon onion powder

Combine all the ingredients until well blended. Chill until ready to serve.

Makes ⅔ cup dressing. Each tablespoon has 8 calories.

HERB DRESSING

¼ **cup tarragon vinegar**
¼ **cup water**
2 **tablespoons salad oil**
1 **garlic clove, minced**
¼ **teaspoon dried oregano**
¼ **teaspoon dried thyme**
⅛ **teaspoon freshly ground black pepper**

Combine all the ingredients in a screw-top jar and shake well. Store, covered, in the refrigerator until ready to use. Shake well before using.

Makes about ⅔ cup of dressing. Each tablespoon has 17 calories.

Note: The recipe may be doubled and stored in the refrigerator for several weeks. Serve as a low-calorie salad dressing on crisp greens.

DILLED BUTTERMILK DRESSING

¼ **cup buttermilk**
½ **teaspoon dried dill**
⅛ **teaspoon celery seed**
⅛ **teaspoon freshly ground black pepper**

Combine all the ingredients in a screw-top jar and mix well. Store in a refrigerator until ready to use. Shake well before using.

Makes 2 servings. Each tablespoon has 13 calories.

Note: The recipe may be halved to serve 1 or doubled to serve 4. Serve with crisp greens.

CELERY SEED–YOGURT DRESSING

- ½ cup plain low-fat yogurt
- 2 tablespoons ketchup
- 1 teaspoon sugar
- 2 tablespoons fresh lemon juice
- 1 tablespoon grated onion
- ½ teaspoon paprika
- ½ teaspoon celery seed

Stir the yogurt and ketchup together. Add the remaining ingredients and mix well.

Makes almost 1 cup dressing. Each tablespoon has about 10 calories.

CUCUMBER–YOGURT DRESSING

- 1 cup plain low-fat yogurt
- ½ cup finely diced cucumber, peeled
- ¼ teaspoon Worcestershire sauce
- ½ teaspoon dried dill
- 2 tablespoons fresh lemon juice

Combine all the ingredients and mix well. Chill for several hours before using.

Makes 1⅔ cups dressing. Each tablespoon has 5 calories.

YOGURT–BLUE CHEESE DRESSING

   ½ cup plain low-fat yogurt
   2 tablespoons crumbled blue cheese
   1 small garlic clove, minced
   ¼ teaspoon dried tarragon

Combine all the ingredients and mix well. Store in the refrigerator until ready to serve.

Makes ⅔ cup dressing. Each tablespoon has 13 calories.

Note: Serve with crisp greens. You can also omit the garlic and serve as a fruit salad dressing.

SPICY YOGURT DRESSING

   1 cup plain low-fat yogurt
   2 ounces blue cheese, crumbled
   2 tablespoons fresh lemon juice
   1 teaspoon Worcestershire sauce
   ½ teaspoon garlic powder
   ⅛ teaspoon dry mustard
   ⅛ teaspoon paprika

Mash the yogurt and blue cheese together until almost smooth. Add the lemon juice, Worcestershire sauce, garlic powder, mustard, and paprika. Mix well. Chill until ready to use.

Makes 1¼ cups dressing. Each tablespoon has 20 calories.

Twelve

Nutritious Breakfasts

Breakfast sets you up with energy for the day. It may be the most important meal you eat, because it provides the fuel for four or more morning hours that are often essential to get work done well.

You should eat only a few eggs a week. While they are high in cholesterol, eggs also contain valuable nutrients and pack a wallop of protein into 75 calories. Don't prepare them with butter or fat—use a nonstick frying pan if you plan to make an omelet or scramble them. Otherwise, poach, boil, or bake the eggs as directed in many of the recipes which follow.

At other times, a good wholesome cooked cereal like Grandma used to put on the table is still a wise choice. Don't add butter or sugar. A dash of cinnamon can give hot cereal a wonderful flavor for no calories at all. Use only skim milk if you want to thin the consistency of the cereal, or use a teaspoon of frozen apple juice concentrate which has a great sweetening power and very pleasant flavor for very few calories.

If you prefer cold breakfast cereal, choose one that is not presweetened. Preferably, choose one that is high in bulk, such as shredded wheat, Raisin Bran, or All-Bran. Add a half a sliced banana or unsweetened berries when in season, and use only skim milk and no sugar.

An excellent breakfast is low-fat cottage cheese with half a sliced banana or fresh berries in season. It gives you a lot of protein for very few calories.

Do add a half glass of citrus juice, pineapple juice, or apple juice to your breakfast menu. Or eat a melon wedge, fresh berries in season, half a grapefruit, or half a sliced orange.

When toast is suggested on the menu, make it from whole grain bread. Do not use butter, but you may spread a thin layer of dietetic jelly over the toast if you can't eat it plain.

Use only skim milk in your breakfast beverage. Cream may taste better but so does everything that has a high-fat content. Fat does have a high degree of satiety, but it manages to stick to hips like glue!

BAKED EGG IN ENGLISH MUFFIN

½ **whole wheat English muffin**
1 **egg**
¼ **teaspoon dried dill**
  Dash of freshly ground black pepper

Scoop out the soft part of the muffin and discard it. Break the egg into muffin. Sprinkle with dill and pepper. Put on a small cookie sheet or in a baking dish and bake in a 350-degree oven for 15 minutes, or until done to taste.

Makes 1 serving. Each serving has 125 calories.

POACHED EGG ON RAISIN TOAST

1 cup water
1 teaspoon white vinegar
1 egg
1 slice toasted raisin bread

Bring the water to a boil in a small frying pan. Add the vinegar. Break the egg into the water and quickly spoon the wisps of white over the egg. Turn heat to simmer and cook for 3 to 4 minutes. Remove the poached egg with a slotted spoon and place it on the toasted raisin bread.

Makes 1 serving. Each serving has 135 calories.

COTTAGE CHEESE OMELET

1 egg, beaten
2 tablespoons low-fat cottage cheese
1 teaspoon chopped fresh or frozen chives

Cook the egg in a nonstick frying pan, pushing the solidified egg to the center to let the liquid run out to the edges and set. Flip onto a plate. Spread the cottage cheese over half the omelet and cover with the other half. Sprinkle with the chopped chives.

Makes 1 serving. Each serving has 100 calories.

RANCH OMELET

   1 small tomato, diced
 ½ green bell pepper, diced
   1 small onion, diced
   1 tablespoon water
   2 eggs
 ¼ teaspoon dried oregano
   Dash of freshly ground black pepper

Put the diced tomato, green pepper, and onion in a large nonstick frying pan. Add the water and simmer the vegetables for 2 to 3 minutes, or until they are tender. Beat the eggs with the oregano and pepper and pour over the vegetables in the frying pan. Cover and cook for 3 to 4 minutes, or until the eggs are solidified.

Makes 1 serving. Each serving has 225 calories.

JELLY ROLL OMELET

   2 eggs
   1 tablespoon water
   2 tablespoons dietetic jelly

Beat the eggs and water together. Pour into a nonstick frying pan and cook over medium heat. Push the solidified egg to the center, allowing the liquid egg to run to the rim. Flip the omelet out onto a warm plate. Spread the dietetic jelly over the top of the omelet and roll up.

Makes 2 servings. Each serving has 80 calories.

FRAMED EGG

1 **slice rye bread**
1 **egg**
   Dash of paprika

Tear out the center of the rye bread and discard it. Put the rye crust in a nonstick frying pan. Break the egg into the center. Sprinkle with the paprika. Cover the pan and cook for 3 to 4 minutes, or until done to your taste.

Makes 1 serving. Each serving has 100 calories.

FRENCH TOAST

1 **egg**
2 **tablespoons skim milk**
¼ **teaspoon vanilla extract**
2 **slices day old bread**
¼ **teaspoon ground cinnamon**

Beat the egg. Add the skim milk and vanilla and beat well. Dip each slice of bread into the egg mixture to coat well. Brown in a nonstick frying pan. Turn and brown the other side. Remove to a warm plate and sprinkle with cinnamon.

Makes 2 servings. Each serving has 108 calories.

CHEESE DANISH

  1 slice raisin bread
  2 tablespoons low-fat cottage cheese
  ¼ teaspoon ground cinnamon
  ¼ teaspoon grated lemon rind

Top the raisin bread with a layer of cottage cheese. Sprinkle with cinnamon and grated lemon peel. Broil for 1 to 2 minutes, or until the cheese is hot.

Makes 1 serving. Each serving has 85 calories.

CANTALOUPE SURPRISE

  ½ cantaloupe
  ½ cup low-fat cottage cheese
  ½ banana, sliced
  1 tablespoon lemon low-fat yogurt

Fill the melon half with the cottage cheese. Add a ring of sliced bananas around the edge. Top with the lemon yogurt.

Makes 1 serving. Each serving has 185 calories.

OATMEAL WITH RAISINS

½ **cup instant oatmeal**
 Boiling water
2 **tablespoons seedless raisins**
¼ **teaspoon ground cinnamon**
2 **tablespoons skim milk**

Put the instant oatmeal in a bowl. Add just enough boiling water to make a palatable consistency. Add the raisins, cinnamon, and skim milk. Stir.

Makes 1 serving. Each serving has 140 calories.

GRITS WITH ALMONDS

½ **cup instant grits**
 Boiling water
1 **tablespoon thawed apple juice concentrate**
1 **tablespoon slivered almonds**

Put the instant grits in a bowl. Add just enough boiling water to make a palatable consistency. Add the apple juice concentrate and stir through. Top with the slivered almonds.

Makes 1 serving. Each serving has 100 calories.

Thirteen

Low-Calorie Desserts

The best dessert you can eat is a piece of fresh fruit, such as an apple, pear, banana, peach, nectarine, or a dish of fresh berries.

Next best is to poach or bake an apple or pear without added sugar. Or to broil half a grapefruit. Or to put in a stock of canned unsweetened fruit and enjoy the ease of opening and serving them. Or to measure out a strict ¼ cup of frozen yogurt or vanilla ice milk on half of an unsweetened peach, once in a while.

There are bound to be times when you will really crave a cookie, or want to make a special dessert for company and yet want to follow this low-calorie diet. Here is a chapter of dessert recipes that have just the sleight of hand you need to make those tempting dreams come true.

Please remember that fat and sugar are just what you don't need if you want to lose weight. Pay particular attention to the serving sizes of portions, so you don't destroy the value of the entire diet plan. This chapter is included so you won't feel completely deprived. But then again, you are going to be indulging in delectable pasta dishes for two weeks or more and that's like having your cake and eating it too!

AMBROSIA

½ **grapefruit**
1 **orange**
6 **strawberries**
1 **tablespoon flaked coconut**

Cut the grapefruit and orange into segments. Remove all the membranes. Cut the strawberries in half and add to cut fruit. Spoon into 2 dessert dishes and top with the flaked coconut.

Makes 2 servings. Each serving has 89 calories.

APPLESAUCE

6 **unpeeled and uncored apples, cut up**
1 **cup water**
2 **tablespoons sugar**
1 **tablespoon lemon lemon juice**

Put the cut up apples into a saucepan. Add the water, sugar, and lemon juice. Cover and simmer for 20 minutes, or until the apples are very soft. Work through a food mill to purée, removing the skins and seeds.

Makes 8 servings. Each serving has 66 calories.

BAKED APPLES

2 baking apples
1 teaspoon soft brown sugar
2 teaspoons raisins

Core the apples, leaving bottom stem end intact. Put the apples, open end up, in a baking dish. Fill the centers with the brown sugar and raisins. Pour ½ inch of water around the apples. Bake in a 400-degree oven for 35 to 40 minutes, or until the apples are tender. Serve hot or cold.

Makes 2 servings. Each serving has 99 calories.

BROILED BANANAS

2 bananas
1 tablespoon fresh lemon juice
2 teaspoons honey

Peel bananas and cut them in half lengthwise; if very long, cut in half crosswise as well. Sprinkle with the lemon juice and arrange in a buttered baking pan with rounded sides up. Brush with the honey. Broil for 5 minutes, or until lightly browned.

Makes 2 servings. Each serving has 107 calories.

BROILED GRAPEFRUIT

1 **grapefruit, halved**
2 **teaspoons brown sugar**
¼ **teaspoon ground cinnamon**

Cut around the segments of the grapefruit halves. Sprinkle the top of each half with brown sugar and cinnamon. Broil the grapefruit for about 6 minutes, or until lightly browned on top. Serve hot.

Makes 2 servings. Each serving has 63 calories.

POACHED PEARS

½ **cup water**
2 **tablespoons sugar**
1 **tablespoon fresh lemon juice**
2 **fresh pears, peeled, halved, and cored**

Cook the water, sugar, and lemon juice together in a saucepan until the sugar dissolves. Add the pear halves. Cover and simmer until they are tender, about 15 minutes. Chill and serve.

Makes 2 servings. Each serving has 148 calories.

FRUIT COMPOTE

1   8-ounce can unsweetened peaches
1   8-ounce can unsweetened pears
¼   cup fresh orange juice
½   teaspoon grated lemon rind
½   teaspoon honey

Drain the juice from the canned fruit into a saucepan. Add the orange juice, lemon rind, and honey. Cook over low heat until mixture is reduced to half. Put the peaches and pears into a small deep bowl. Pour the cooked juice over all and chill until ready to serve.

Makes 4 servings. Each serving has 50 calories.

STRAWBERRY FLIP

1   cup strawberry halves
¼   cup plain low-fat yogurt
¼   teaspoon vanilla extract
    Dash of ground nutmeg

Divide the strawberries between 2 sherbet glasses, saving 4 halves. Put the 4 strawberry halves into a blender with the yogurt, vanilla extract, and nutmeg. Blend into a smooth sauce. Pour the sauce over strawberries and serve.

Makes 2 servings. Each serving has 43 calories.

PEACH MELBA

2 canned unsweetened peach halves
½ cup vanilla ice cream
¼ cup fresh or frozen raspberries, puréed

Arrange the peach halves cut side up in dessert dishes. Top with a small scoop of vanilla ice cream. Pour the raspberry purée over all.

Makes 2 servings. Each serving has 79 calories.

BISQUE TORTONI

1 cup nonfat dry milk powder
¾ cup water
2 tablespoons fresh lemon juice
2 tablespoons sugar
1 teaspoon vanilla extract
1 tablespoon ground almonds
1 egg white

Using an electric beater, beat the dry milk powder and water together until it thickens. Add the lemon juice, sugar, vanilla extract, and almonds. Beat well. In a separate bowl with clean beaters, beat the egg white until stiff peaks form. Fold into the milk mixture. Spoon into 6 small cupcake double-paper liners. Freeze.

Makes 6 servings. Each serving has 94 calories.

ORANGE SHERBET

1 6-ounce can frozen orange juice
1 ¾ cups cold water
½ cup nonfat dry milk powder
1 tablespoon sugar

Put the juice concentrate into a mixing bowl. Add the water, dry milk powder, and sugar. Beat until well blended. Pour into an ice cube tray and freeze until half frozen, 1 to 2 hours. Transfer to a large chilled mixing bowl and beat at low speed until the mixture is softened; then beat on high speed for 3 to 5 minutes, or until the mixture is creamy but not liquid. Pour into a freezer container or back into the ice cube tray and freeze until firm.

Makes 6 servings. Each serving has 104 calories.

FROZEN FRESH FRUIT PURÉE

1 cup strawberries
1 banana

Wash and hull the strawberries and put them in an electric food processor. Add the peeled banana. Process until smooth. Freeze.

Makes 2 servings. Each serving has 73 calories.

Note: The recipe may be halved to serve 1 or doubled to serve 4. Serve with a sprinkling of shredded coconut, if desired.

LEMON ICE

½ **envelope (1 ½ teaspoons) unflavored gelatin**
½ **cup sugar**
¾ **cup water**
 3 **egg whites**
½ **cup fresh lemon juice**

Combine the gelatin and ¼ cup sugar in a saucepan. Blend in the water, stirring until smooth. Bring the mixture to a boil, stirring, until the gelatin has dissolved. Remove from the heat. Beat the egg whites at high speed until soft peaks form. Add the remaining sugar gradually, continuing to beat until all the sugar is used and the whites are stiff, but not dry. Continue beating, adding the warm mixture in a thin steady stream. Beat in the lemon juice. Pour into two ice cube trays and freeze until mushy, stirring once or twice. When the mixture is evenly frozen to the mushy stage, transfer to a chilled mixing bowl. With chilled beaters, beat at high speed until smooth and light. Return to the freezer until firm.

Makes 8 servings. Each serving has 52 calories.

CITRUS MINTED YOGURT

1 **cup plain low-fat yogurt**
1 **teaspoon grated orange rind**
1 **teaspoon grated lemon rind**
1 **teaspoon chopped fresh mint leaves**
¼ **teaspoon vanilla extract**

Combine all the ingredients and mix well. Chill. Spoon into dessert dishes to serve.

Makes 2 servings. Each serving has 62 calories.

APRICOT FLUFF

1 5-ounce jar strained apricots for babies
1 teaspoon honey
1 teaspoon vanilla extract
1 teaspoon fresh lemon juice
1 teaspoon grated lemon rind
1 teaspoon unflavored gelatin
1 tablespoon cold water
2 egg whites

Stir together the strained apricots, honey, vanilla, lemon juice, and lemon rind. Soften the gelatin in the cold water; then dissolve it over hot water in a double boiler. Beat the egg whites until frothy. Add the gelatin and beat until very stiff. Fold into the apricot mixture and spoon into wineglasses. Chill.

Makes 4 servings. Each serving has 43 calories.

CITRUS GELATIN

can unsweetened grapefruit sections
Orange juice
1 envelope unflavored gelatin
1 cup water

Drain the grapefruit and set aside. Measure the drained grapefruit juice and add enough orange juice to make 1 cup. Soften the gelatin in the juice mixture. Stir over low heat until dissolved. Add the water. Add the grapefruit sections. Spoon into 6 dessert cups. Chill until set.

Makes 6 servings. Each serving has 35 calories.

RASPBERRY SNOW

  1 **envelope unflavored gelatin**
  ½ **cup cold water**
  1 **10-ounce package frozen unsweetened raspberries, thawed**
      Artificial sweetener equivalent to ½ cup sugar
  1 **teaspoon grated lemon rind**
  1 **teaspoon fresh lemon juice**
  2 **egg whites**

Sprinkle the gelatin over the cold water in a saucepan. Place over low heat and stir constantly until the gelatin dissolves, about 3 minutes. Remove from the heat. Purée the raspberries in an electric blender, food processor, or by rubbing through a sieve. Add to the dissolved gelatin with the sweetener, lemon rind, and lemon juice. Chill, stirring occasionally, until the mixture mounds slightly when dropped from a spoon. Add to the egg whites in a chilled bowl and beat with an electric mixer until light and fluffy, about 10 minutes. Turn into a mold or into 8 individual dessert dishes. Chill until set, 2 to 3 hours.

Makes 8 servings. Each serving has 45 calories.

ORANGE WHIP

    1 envelope unflavored gelatin
   ½ cup cold water
    1 6-ounce can frozen orange juice concentrate
       Artificial sweetener equivalent to ½ cup sugar
    2 egg whites
   ½ cup nonfat dry milk powder
   ½ cup ice water

Sprinkle the gelatin over ½ cup of cold water in a saucepan. Cook and stir until the gelatin dissolves, 2 to 3 minutes. Remove from the heat. Add the frozen orange juice concentrate and artificial sweetener to the dissolved gelatin and stir until melted. Chill, stirring occasionally, until the mixture thickens and mounds slightly when dropped from a spoon. Beat the egg whites until stiff peaks form. Fold into the orange mixture. Combine the dry milk powder and ice water, and, using the same beaters, beat until firm peaks form, about 5 minutes. Fold into the orange mixture. Spoon into small dessert dishes, piling the mixture high. Chill until set.

Makes 10 ½-cup servings. Each serving has 66 calories.

SPICED COFFEE JELLY

1 envelope unflavored gelatin
1 ¾ cups cold water
2 tablespoons instant coffee powder
1 cinnamon stick
3 whole cloves
⅓ cup sugar

Soften the gelatin in ½ cup of the cold water. Put the remaining water, the coffee powder, cinnamon, and cloves in a saucepan. Simmer for 5 minutes. Remove the cinnamon stick and cloves. Add the softened gelatin mixture and stir until dissolved. Stir in the sugar. Pour into 4 wineglasses. Chill until firm. Serve with a dollop of low-calorie whipped topping, if desired.

Makes 4 servings. Each serving has 64 calories.

PRUNE WHIP

2 ounces pitted prunes
1 teaspoon fresh lemon juice
1 tablespoon sugar
1 egg white

Put the prunes in a small saucepan and cover with water. Cook until soft. Remove the prunes with a slotted spoon and purée in an electric blender or food processor. Discard the cooking water. Add the lemon juice and sugar to the puréed prunes. Beat the egg white until stiff peaks form and fold into the prune mixture. Spoon into individual stemmed glasses and chill.

Makes 2 servings. Each serving has 108 calories.

SUGAR-FREE LEMON COOKIES

    ½ cup butter or margarine
    1 tablespoon liquid artificial sweetener   .
    1 egg, slightly beaten
    1 teaspoon vanilla extract
    1 teaspoon grated lemon rind
    1 cup all-purpose flour
    ¾ teaspoon baking soda
    ¼ teaspoon salt

Preheat the oven to 375 degrees. Beat the butter in a mixing bowl
until fluffy. Add the liquid sweetener, egg, vanilla, and lemon peel
and beat well. Combine the flour, baking soda, and salt and add to
creamed mixture. Drop by teaspoon onto an ungreased cookie
sheet and press flat with a fork. Bake for 8 minutes, or until lightly
browned.   *Makes 3 dozen cookies. Each cookie has about 39 calories.*

CORN FLAKE MACAROONS

    2 egg whites
    ½ teaspoon salt
    1 cup sugar
    ¼ teaspoon almond extract
    1 cup shredded coconut
    2 cups corn flakes

Preheat the oven to 350 degrees. Beat the egg whites until foamy
and add the salt. Gradually add the sugar while beating constantly
until stiff peaks form. Add the almond extract. Fold in the shredded
coconut and corn flakes. Drop by teaspoons onto a greased cookie
sheet about 2 inches apart. Bake for 15 minutes, or until lightly
browned. Remove the cookies immediately.
        Makes about 3½ dozen cookies. Each cookie has about 40 calories.

SUGAR-FREE CHOCOLATE COOKIES

   $\frac{1}{2}$ cup butter or margarine
       Granulated sugar substitute to equal $\frac{3}{4}$ cup sugar
   1 egg
   1 teaspoon vanilla extract
1 $\frac{1}{4}$ cups cake flour
   $\frac{1}{4}$ cup cocoa powder
   $\frac{3}{4}$ teaspoon baking soda
   $\frac{1}{8}$ teaspoon salt
   2 tablespoons milk

Beat the butter and sugar substitute until fluffy. Add the egg and vanilla and beat well. Combine the flour, cocoa, baking soda, and salt. Add alternately with the milk to the batter. Mix well. Shape the dough into a roll 1 $\frac{1}{2}$ inches in diameter. Wrap in wax paper and chill for several hours or overnight. When ready to bake, preheat the oven to 350 degrees. Slice the dough into $\frac{1}{8}$-inch-thick rounds. Place on an ungreased cookie sheet. Bake for 8 to 10 minutes.

Makes 3 dozen cookies. Each cookie has about 42 calories.

CRISP CORN FLAKE COOKIES

⅔ cup solid shortening
1 cup light brown sugar
1 egg, beaten
1 teaspoon vanilla extract
1 cup all-purpose flour
½ teaspoon baking soda
¼ teaspoon salt
2 cups corn flakes

Preheat the oven to 350 degrees. Beat the shortening and sugar until fluffy. Add the egg and vanilla and beat well. Mix together the flour, baking soda, and salt and stir into the batter. Stir in the corn flakes. Drop the dough by teaspoon onto a greased cookie sheet, about 2 inches apart. Bake for 10 to 15 minutes, or until lightly browned. Remove from the cookie sheet while still warm. Cool on a rack.

Makes about 4 dozen cookies. Each cookie has about 55 calories.

OATMEAL COOKIES

¾ cup solid shortening
  1 cup confectioners' sugar
¼ cup skim milk
  2 teaspoons vanilla extract
1¾ cups all-purpose flour
¾ teaspoon salt
  1 cup uncooked oatmeal

Preheat the oven to 350 degrees. Beat the shortening until creamy. Add the sugar and beat until fluffy. Add the skim milk and vanilla and beat well. Combine the flour, salt, and oatmeal. Add gradually to the batter to make a stiff dough. Shape the dough into balls about 1 inch in diameter. Place about 2 inches apart on an ungreased cookie sheet. Bake for 25 minutes, or until lightly browned. Remove from the cookie sheet while still warm. Cool on a rack.

Makes about 4 dozen cookies. Each cookie has about 70 calories.

COCONUT MERINGUE COOKIES

   2 **egg whites**
   ¼ **teaspoon salt**
   ¼ **cup sugar**
   ½ **teaspoon almond extract**
   ¼ **cup flaked coconut**

Beat the egg whites and salt until soft peaks form. Add sugar gradually while beating until mixture is stiff. Add the almond extract and coconut. Drop by spoonfuls onto a nonstick cookie sheet. Bake for about 40 minutes in a slow 250-degree oven; then turn off the heat. Let the oven cool before removing the cookies. Store in a covered canister.

Makes about 1 ½ dozen cookies. Each cookie has about 23 calories.

OATMEAL–RAISIN COOKIES

  1 **cup all-purpose flour**
1 ¼ **teaspoons baking powder**
  ½ **teaspoon baking soda**
  ½ **teaspoon salt**
  ½ **cup solid shortening**
  1 **cup light brown sugar**
  1 **egg**
  1 **teaspoon vanilla extract**
1 ½ **cups uncooked quick-cooking oatmeal**
  ½ **cup seedless raisins**

Mix the flour, baking powder, baking soda, and salt together. Beat the shortening and sugar until fluffy. Add the egg and vanilla and beat well. Mix in the flour mixture. Mix in the oatmeal and raisins. Chill the dough for 1 hour. Preheat the oven to 350 degrees. Shape the dough into balls about 1 inch in diameter. Place about 2 inches apart on an ungreased cookie sheet. Bake for 15 minutes, or until browned. Remove from the cookie sheet while still warm and cool on a rack.

Makes 4 dozen cookies. Each cookie has about 60 calories.

CHOCOLATE NUT DROPS

1 12-ounce package chocolate chips
1 14-ounce can sweetened condensed milk
2 cups uncooked quick-cooking oatmeal
¼ teaspoon salt
2 teaspoons vanilla extract
⅔ cup toasted almonds or pecan halves

Melt the chocolate chips in the top of a double boiler over hot water or in a microwave oven. Remove the double boiler from the heat. Add the remaining ingredients, except nuts. Keep the mixture hot over hot water while dropping teaspoons of the dough onto wax paper on a cookie sheet. Top each cookie with an almond or pecan half. Refrigerate until set. Store in the refrigerator until used.

Makes about 6 dozen cookies. Each cookie has about 60 calories.

SUGAR-FREE CHOCOLATE CHEESECAKE

⅔ cup milk
1 envelope unflavored gelatin
2 eggs, separated
¼ cup unsweetened pure cocoa powder
Granulated sugar substitute to equal ½ cup sugar
2 teaspoons vanilla extract
1¾ cups part skim ricotta

Combine the milk and gelatin in a small saucepan, stirring to soften gelatin. Heat and stir until the gelatin has dissolved. Cool slightly. Pour into a mixing bowl. Add the egg yolks, cocoa, sugar substitute, and vanilla. Beat well. Add the ricotta and beat until smooth. Chill, stirring occasionally, until the mixture mounds from a spoon. Beat the egg whites until stiff peaks form. Carefully fold the beaten egg whites into the chocolate mixture. Pour into an 8-inch springform pan. Chill for several hours or overnight.

Makes 12 servings. Each serving has about 98 calories.

General Calorie Counts

DAIRY PRODUCTS

Cheeses:

American, Cheddar type	1 oz.	115
	1″ cube	70
	½ cup, grated	225
American processed, Cheddar type	1 oz.	105
Blue-mold (Roquefort)	″	105
Cottage, creamed	2 tbsps.	30
Cottage, not creamed	″	25
Cream cheese	″	105
Parmesan, dry, grated	″	40
Swiss	1 oz.	105

Fluid Milk:

Buttermilk	1 cup	90
Condensed, sweetened (undiluted)	½ cup	490
Evaporated (undiluted)	½ cup	170
Half-and-half (milk and cream)	1 cup	330
	1 tbsp.	20
Skim	1 cup	90
Whole	1 cup	165

Milk Beverages:

Cocoa (all milk)	1 cup	235
Chocolate-flavored milk drink	"	190
Chocolate milk shake	12 oz.	520
Malted milk	1 cup	280

Others:

Butter	1 tbsp.	100
Cream, light	"	35
Cream, heavy whipping	"	55
Ice cream, plain	3 ½ oz.	130
Ice cream soda, chocolate	1 glass	455
Ice milk	½ cup	140
Yogurt (partially skim milk)	1 cup	120

MEATS AND POULTRY
(Cooked, without bone)

Beef:

Beef and vegetable stew	½ cup	90
Beef potpie, baked	1 pie, 4 ¼ " dia.	460
Corned beef, canned	3 oz.	180
Corned beef hash, canned	"	120
Dried beef, chipped	2 oz.	115
Hamburger		
Regular ground beef	3 oz. patty	245
Lean ground round	"	185
Meat loaf	2 oz.	115
Oven roast		
Lean and fat	3 oz.	220
Lean only	2 ½ oz.	130
Pot roast or braised		
Lean and fat	3 oz.	245
Lean only	2 ½ oz.	140

Steak, broiled
Lean and fat	3 oz.	330
Lean only	2 oz.	115

Veal:
Cutlet, broiled (meat only)	3 oz.	185

Chicken:
Broiled	3 oz.	185
Canned	½ cup	190
Fried	½ breast	215
	Thigh and drumstick	245

Lamb:
Chop
Lean and fat	4 oz.	405
Lean only	2 ⅗ oz.	140

Roast leg
Lean and fat	3 oz.	235
Lean only	2 ½ oz.	130

Pork:
Bacon, broiled	2 thin slices	95
Boiled ham	2 oz.	170

Chop
Lean and fat	2 ⅓ oz.	260
Lean only	2 oz.	130

Ham, cured
Lean and fat	3 oz.	290
Lean only	2 ⅕ oz.	125

Roast loin
Lean and fat	3 oz.	310
Lean only	2 ⅖ oz.	175
Spiced ham, canned	2 oz.	165

Sausage and Variety Meats:

Bologna sausage	2 oz.	170
Liver sausage	″	175
Pork sausage, bulk	2 oz. patty	170
Vienna sausage, canned	2 oz.	135
Beef liver, fried	2 oz.	120
Beef tongue, boiled	3 oz.	205
Frankfurter	Each	155

FISH AND SHELLFISH

Bluefish, baked	3 oz.	135
Clams, shelled		
Raw, meat only	″	70
Canned, clams and juice	″	45
Crabmeat	″	90
Fish sticks	4 oz.	200
Haddock, fried	3 oz.	135
Mackerel		
Broiled	″	200
Canned	″	155
Ocean perch, fried	″	195
Oysters, raw	6 to 10	80
Salmon		
Broiled	4 oz.	205
Canned (pink)	3 oz.	120
Sardines, canned in oil	″	180
Shrimp, canned	″	110
Tuna, canned in oil	″	170

EGGS

Boiled	1 large	80
Fried	"	100
Poached	"	80
Scrambled or omelet	"	110

NUTS

Almonds, shelled	15 nuts	105
Brazil nuts, broken	2 tbsps.	115
Cashew nuts, roasted	5 nuts	95
Coconut, shredded	2 tbsps.	40
Peanut butter	1 tbsp.	90
Peanuts, roasted, shelled	2 tbsps.	105
Pecans, shelled	12 halves	90
Walnuts, shelled		
Black	2 tbsps.	100
English	10 halves	80

VEGETABLES

Asparagus	6 spears	20
Beans, dried		
Red kidney, cooked	½ cup	115
Lima, cooked	"	130
Baked		
With pork	"	165
Without pork	"	160
Beans, fresh		
Lima	½ cup	75
Snap, green or wax	"	15
Beet greens, cooked	"	20

Beets	"	35
Broccoli	"	20
Brussels sprouts	"	30
Cabbage		
Coleslaw (with dressing)	"	50
Cooked	"	20
Raw	"	10
Carrots	"	20
Cauliflower	"	15
Celery	2 large stalks	10
Chard	½ cup	25
Collards	"	40
Corn, cooked	"	85
Corn on cob	1 ear	65
Cress, garden	½ cup	35
Cucumbers	6 slices	5
Kale	½ cup	20
Kohlrabi	"	25
Lettuce	3 leaves	5
Mushrooms, canned	½ cup	15
Mustard greens	"	15
Okra, cooked	4 pods	15
Onions		
Cooked	½ cup	40
Raw	1 medium sized	50
Parsnips, cooked	½ cup	50
Peas, green	"	60
Peppers, bell	1 medium	15
Potatoes		
Baked or boiled	"	90
Chips	10 medium	110
French-fried	10 pieces	155
Hash-browned	½ cup	235
Mashed with milk	"	70
Pan-fried	"	240

Radishes	4 small	10
Sauerkraut, canned	½ cup	15
Spinach	"	20
Squash		
Summer	½ cup	20
Winter, baked	"	50
Sweet potatoes		
Baked	1 medium	155
Canned	½ cup	120
Tomatoes		
Cooked or canned	½ cup	25
Raw	1 medium	30
Tomato juice	½ cup	25
Turnip greens	"	20
Turnips, cooked	"	20

FRUITS

Apple juice	½ cup	60
Applesauce		
Sweetened	"	90
Unsweetened	"	50
Apples, raw	1 medium	70
Apricots		
Canned, syrup pack	½ cup	110
Canned, water pack	"	45
Dried, cooked, unsweetened	"	120
Frozen, sweetened	"	125
Raw	3	55
Avocados	½ 10-oz. size	185
Bananas, raw	1 medium	85

Berries

Blackberries, raw	½ cup	40
Blueberries, raw	"	45
Raspberries, raw	"	35
Frozen, sweetened	"	120
Strawberries, raw	"	30
Frozen, sweetened	"	120
Cantaloupe, raw	½ melon, 5″ dia.	40

Cherries

Canned red, sour, pitted	½ cup	55
Raw	"	30
Cranberry sauce, sweetened	1 tbsp.	30

Cranberry juice

cocktail	½ cup	70
Dates	"	250

Figs

Canned, heavy syrup	½ cup	110
Dried	1 large	60
Raw	3 small	90
Fruit cocktail, canned in syrup	½ cup	100

Grapefruit

Canned syrup pack	½ cup	80
Canned water pack	"	35
Raw	½ medium	50

Grapefruit juice

Sweetened	½ cup	65
Unsweetened	"	50
Grape juice, bottled	½ cup	75
Grapes	3½ oz.	45
Honeydew melon	2″ × 7″ wedge	50
Lemon juice	½ cup	30
	1 tbsp.	5

Lemonade	½ cup	65
Orange juice	″	60
Oranges, raw	1 orange	70
Peaches		
Canned, syrup pack	½ cup	100
Canned, water pack	″	40
Dried, cooked, unsweetened	″	110
Frozen, sweetened	″	105
Raw	1 medium	35
Pears		
Canned in heavy syrup	½ cup	100
Raw	1 pear	100
Pineapple		
Canned, syrup pack	½ cup (2 slices)	100
Raw	½ cup, diced	35
Pineapple juice	½ cup	60
Plums		
Canned, syrup pack	″	90
Raw	1 plum	30
Prune juice, canned	½ cup	85
Prunes, dried cooked		
Sweetened	9 prunes	260
Unsweetened	″	150
Raisins, dried	½ cup	230
Rhubarb, cooked,		
sweetened	″	190
Tangerine, raw	1 medium	40
Tangerine juice,		
canned	½ cup	50
Watermelon, raw	4″ × 8″ wedge	120

BREADS AND CEREALS

Cracked wheat	slice	60
Raisin	"	60
Rye	"	55
White	"	60
Whole Wheat	"	55

Other Baked Goods:

Baking powder biscuit	each	130
Bran muffins	"	125
Buckwheat cakes	4″ dia.	45
Corn muffins	each	155
Graham crackers	2 medium	55
Hard round rolls	each	160
Pancakes, wheat	4″ dia.	60
Pizza (cheese)	⅛, 14″ pie	180
Plain muffins	each	135
Plain pan rolls	"	115
Pretzels	5 sticks	20
Rye wafers	2	45
Saltines	2	35
Soda crackers	2	45
Sweet pan rolls	each	135
Waffles	4½″ × 5½″	240

Cereals and Other Grain Products:

Bran flakes (40% bran)	1 oz.	85
Corn and soy shreds	"	100
Corn flakes	"	110
Corn grits, cooked	¾ cup	90
Corn, puffed, presweetened	1 oz.	110
Farina, cooked	¾ cup	80
Macaroni and cheese	½ cup	240
Macaroni, cooked	¾ cup	115

Noodles, cooked	¾ cup	150
Oat cereal	1 ounce	115
Oatmeal, cooked	¾ cup	110
Rice, cooked	"	150
Rice flakes	1 cup	115
Rice, puffed	"	55
Spaghetti, cooked	¾ cup	115
Spaghetti in tomato sauce, with cheese	"	160
Spaghetti with meat sauce	"	215
Wheat flakes	¾ cup	100
Wheat flours		
All-purpose flour	¾ cup sifted	300
Whole wheat	¾ cup	300
Wheat germ	"	185
Wheat, puffed	1 oz.	100
Wheat, puffed, presweetened	"	105
Wheat, rolled, cooked	¾ cup	130
Wheat, shredded, plain	1 oz.	100

FATS, OILS, AND RELATED PRODUCTS

Cooking fats		
Lard	1 tbsp.	135
Vegetable	"	110
Margarine	"	100
Salad or cooking oils	"	125

Salad Dressings:

Blue cheese, French	1 tbsp.	90
French	"	60
Home-cooked, boiled	"	30
Low-calorie	"	15
Mayonnaise		
Commercial	"	60
Home-cooked	"	110
Thousand Island	"	75

CANDY, SYRUPS, JAMS, JELLIES

Caramels	1 oz.	120
Chocolate creams	"	110
Chocolate, milk, sweetened,	1 oz. bar	145
Chocolate, milk, sweetened, with almonds	"	150
Chocolate mints	1 oz.	110
Chocolate syrup	1 tbsp.	40
Fudge, chocolate	1 oz.	115
Gumdrops	"	95
Hard candy	"	110
Honey	1 tbsp.	60
Jam, marmalade, preserves	"	55
Jelly	"	50
Jelly beans	1 oz.	65
Marshmallows	"	90
Molasses, cane, light	1 tbsp.	50
Peanut brittle	1 oz.	125
Sugar	1 tsp.	15
Syrup, table blends	1 tbsp.	55

DESSERTS

Apple Betty	½ cup	175
Angel food cake	2" slice	110
Butter cake, plain	3" × 2" × 1½" slice	180
	cupcake	130
Chocolate cake, with fudge icing	2" piece	420
Cookies, plain	3" dia.	110
Cornstarch pudding	½ cup	140
Custard baked	"	140
Doughnut	each	135
Fig bars, small	"	55
Fruit ice	½ cup	75
Fruitcake, dark	2" × 2" × ½" slice	105
Gelatin dessert, plain	½ cup	80

Gingerbread	2″ × 2″ × ½″ slice	180
Pies		
Apple	4″ piece	330
Cherry	″	340
Custard	″	265
Lemon meringue	″	300
Mince	″	340
Pumpkin	″	265
Pound cake	1″ slice	130
Prune whip	½ cup	100
Rennet dessert pudding	″	125
Sherbert	″	120
Sponge cake	2″ piece	115

BEVERAGES

Beer, 4% alcohol	12 oz.	175
Coffee or tea	1 cup	0
Cola type	8 oz.	105
Ginger ale	″	80
Low-calorie type	″	10
Postum	1 cup	5
Sweet wines	3 oz.	120
Whisky, gin, rum:		
100-proof	1½ oz.	125
90-proof	″	110
86-proof	″	105
80-proof	″	100
70-proof	″	85
Wines, table use	3 oz.	70

Index

213